PRAI
NATALIE
LYME

Lyme Light is a heartbreaking and dark-humored memoir with an ending you'll never see coming. Full of startling vulnerability and undeniable charm, this young first time author – Natalie London – had me hooked within pages. Natalie will always have a seat next to me at the Peach Pit.

- Tori Spelling, *Beverly Hills, 90210*

In Natalie London's Lyme Light, the author discovers meaning in illness, wit in despair, imagination in loneliness, companionship in culture, and culture in companionship. Her story is a fine example of the heroine's journey toward the Self.

- Alicia Goranson, *Roseanne*

"I pray we'll wake up on the porch of the Connor house..." This line resonated with me. Whatever the medium, art is able to comfort us and connect us. Natalie's book is a testament to that.

- Laurie Metcalf, *Roseanne*

Lyme Light is a memoir of pain, confusion, helplessness and ultimately, hope. Natalie's journey is heartbreaking, but she deals with it with humor and grace. A truly great read. I loved it.

- Jason Priestley, *Beverly Hills, 90210*

Continued…

lyme light

a memoir by:
NATALIE H.G. LONDON

The Perfect Fort Publishing

This is a work of Non-Fiction

LYME LIGHT

The Perfect Fort/published by arrangement with
the author

ISBN: 0615780598
ISBN-13: 978-0615780597

PRINTED IN THE UNITED STATES OF AMERICA

PROLOGUE

I close my eyes and see the sun shining down on me that day. I could not drive anymore. I could not just watch the beauty fly by while my foot pressed the gas to the floor. The mid-west wind rushing through four open windows was simply not enough. I pulled over the car in the middle of the highway, put it in park, left my flashers on. I walked down that steep hill of thick grass. I felt the warm dirt press against my hands, slip under my fingernails, the barbed wire scratch across my back as I crawled onto the land. I walked across the field, letting the tall blades wrap themselves around my legs. I lied down in it. And in a moment, looking through the lens of a cheap plastic throw away camera, I snapped the picture.

I can still see it when I close my eyes.
I can still feel the sun against my back,

Filling me with light.

1 a picture's worth 56,134 words

June, 2009.

My mom used to sing me lullabies every night before I went to sleep, but never the songs any other kids knew. She sang songs like "We Gotta Get out of This Place" by The Animals and "A World of Our Own," by The Seekers, quietly and perhaps unknowingly, guaranteeing me that someday we would build a place where our sorrows wouldn't follow, where anyone or anything that hurt us would be left behind. There was a world out there where peace of mind was obtainable. "We gotta get outta this place, if it's the last thing we ever do!" looped on playback in my head… started the fire, the nipping at my feet.

As early on as I can remember I created crayon colored blueprints, I took my job seriously I planned our escape. Never underestimate the power of repetition combined with circumstance.

I built up. I built high and I built fast, climbing often on nothing more than the fleetingly firm foundation of packed sand beneath my feet. Even as a kid, I always knew one of two things would eventually happen: I'd make it - I'd grab that world, or the whole thing would collapse in a beat below me. I accepted that.

But never in my wildest dreams did I think this is how I would fall, never did I imagine *this* is how it would end.

These days I only have one song in my head. The calm plea of Elvis Perkins' "Hey wait for me" follows me through the motions. I wake up and listen. I take my pills, I cross them off. Another 20 down. 77 more to go to reach the end of another day. A chart gives me some sense of progress, some structure over these past three years of standing still... three exhausting years of breaking windows and walls.

I walk slowly to the fridge to get the first syringe of Rocephin, warm it up between the palms of my hands. I will need one now, one later. I flick the syringe of saline with my middle finger to catch the bubbles and force them up. I push out the air from the top. I will need two this morning, four later. I push out the air from the heparin. I will need one now, two tonight. I hold the caps between my teeth - pull down the sleeve on my left arm to prep and stare at the foreign object sticking out through my skin – a foreign part of what has always felt like a foreign body - haunting me. A tube to my heart. Access for all. A portal for any demon to come and open while I dream. Let all my blood drain out and leave me dead and dry. Access to my worst fear – a passive death.

I open up the alcohol swabs and cringe at the prospect of the unclean. Of making a mistake. Of shooting bacteria straight to my heart. I pull and the blood rushes into the syringe with deep red swirls as it mixes with the clear saline. I push the blood back in – returning it to my body like the tide. I could keep pulling at anytime.

Direct access to your heart never becomes normal, never feels safe.

SASH: Saline. Antibiotic. Saline. Heparin.

The Rocephin is hardly pushed in before I taste it in my teeth, running up through my blood and around my body, up to even the tiniest vessels in my gums. I can smell it from the inside out. I watch my phone to time the infusion, make sure I don't go too fast and make life even worse. Those little things you can still control. Each minute I check the screen on my phone and I wish it would ring, any distraction. Any call but from the collectors who never give up. I wish I could admire their persistence. Mostly I just don't understand what they expect. I don't have the money. I have nothing more to give.

The IV isn't cold, it isn't comfortable. But it always could be worse. It has been. Now it's just tedious. My body is still in pain but at least my brain is mine again. Exhausted, at least I have slept; there was a time not so long ago when sleep was not possible at all. Every dream I have is a thank you that those days are over, even the nightmares are better than nothing at all. And yes, there are so many nightmares when living in this state, some from the malaria medications I'm on, triple the dosage of what they give to kids around my age heading off for a semester abroad or vacation in a foreign land. I swear, sometimes I think they'll pump me with anything.

Some nightmares don't go away when I wake up.

I smile only rarely now, maybe once or twice a day. I've heard rumors that I once had dimples in my cheeks passed down from my Granddad... but I couldn't tell you where they've gone. In my head I am a soldier of sorts, knee high in mud, my clothes soiled and worn. The places I walk through are bleak, almost black. My only job is to keep walking.

Who I am and how I got here has been easy to forget at times, like a dream. I think I had a past, a life before this, but I'm not really sure anymore. I got a rare telephone call the other day, it was my cousin Gabrielle telling me how much my illness had affected her.

"It makes you think," she explained, "You really have to appreciate what you have when someone you know goes from being so successful, doing all kinds of amazing things, to losing almost everything."

"Absolutely," I answered. "Wait... who?"
"You?" She responded confused.

Oh yeah. I had almost forgotten.

This routine is now my life. I no longer have large goals on a large scale. I no longer do great work for great men. I have a checklist and boxes full of medicine and bandages. I drive myself each day to HBOT (hyperbaric oxygen treatment) to lay in a glass chamber for around two hours. At least I can drive again. Such small joys in life are even routine. I spend my nights falling asleep to pain killers and reruns of *Roseanne*. I schedule HBOT around daily reruns of

Beverly Hills 90210 on the Soap Network. They play on a TV that hovers above the tight glass tube.

This is nothing new. Since I was a child, the genius of *Roseanne* provided me with a complete fictional family. The wonderful cheekiness of Aaron Spelling's original *Beverly Hills 90210* provided me with a complete group of fictional friends... except for Andrea, not even Andrea's friends liked Andrea. I was too young to grow up on the originals but I lived on the daily reruns. By the way, if you don't know what these two shows are, I'm very sorry to hear that you've spent your life in a fallout shelter.

Do you ever think about the amount of human interaction, of physical contact you have during your day? Maybe it's only something you're aware of when it's gone. The tech nurse Jay at the Doctor's office is basically my only human contact – my only hug. That hug, and trying to convince him to admit that he loves being forced to watch *90210*, is now the highlight of every day.

This prior life I have lost, this symbol of how precious and fragile life is that I have apparently become, never gets a chance to cross my mind. I am a machine who rarely has more than a couple thoughts a day that don't concern my treatment; one is always spoken out loud, one is always in my head:

"Ready for 90210?" And *'Hey wait for me.'*

It takes about fifteen minutes to finish the first IV. The liquid is an odd pale yellow, the color of urine that turns a bright red if left out of the fridge too long. It is smart little invention on the part of the chemists that created it, or perhaps an accident of worth - nobody wants to push expired medication into their heart. Rocephin is followed by another saline, then Heparin, a blood thinner, which I wish I didn't need. After more than a year of using it, I only found out recently that Heparin is made with porcine, as in pig. For some reason, there is something not exactly comforting about the thought of having dead pigs running through your veins.

It is only the beginning of my day. I will have another Rocephin IV to do in the evening, the rest of the 77 pills and drops scattered throughout, two hours of hyperbaric oxygen treatment this afternoon, then last but not least I will need a final infusion of Avelox through the IV drip set up next to my bed. It takes a little over an hour and every last piece of energy from my sick body. By the time the last drop hits the line and runs up through my veins, I can't even talk let alone do anything else... except remember. There is one thing that no matter how exhausted I am, I always remember.

Every push, every injection, every pill I must swallow, is intersected by the same slide show over and over again. I remember - that day, that shower. Coming home from driving across the country for the 5th time – from eastern Canada to California. I know where it was. My black car stopped on the side of the highway. I was there, lying in a field in Southern Illinois, taking pictures of rotting cars and abandoned school buses being eaten by deep grass.

Cows running. Crawling on my stomach under barbed wire. Pants torn. The dichotomy, the beauty, the depth and breadth - death and breath of it all, drew me and moved me. It was there.

I should have never gotten out of the car. I should have kept driving.

Every day I remember the shower… thinking for a quick moment there was a spider on my stomach. It had been at least three days since I had showered in Ohio. It was part of that road trip state of mind. Two friends sleeping on the couch seats of my 1983 Oldsmobile during a thunderstorm in a deserted Walmart parking lot. Eating only from a loaf of bread, a jar of peanut butter, and packets of honey taken from a fast food stand. Drinking from jugs of water. That tall grass in southern Illinois… the shower when I finally got home. I screamed as I tried to smack off the spider… in the blur of the water running over my eyes… it was holding on and it wasn't a spider at all.

A tick.

Thick with blood. I ripped it off and watched it circle down the drain. The blood mixed with the water and ran slowly down my stomach.

If only it had taken my blood and given me nothing in return, that would have been okay with me.

With every nightmare, with every deep indescribable

pain, every clench of my teeth, with every step of learning how to walk again, every word – every memory that has disappeared and has now finally returned, with every check off the list, every IV pushed, every pill swallowed…

A photograph.

2 the tornado-man cometh

The first tick bit me in that field in 2003. I had a circular rash on my stomach, a bulls-eye, shortly after that shower. I still have the scar on my stomach from where it clenched my skin - from where its head was left decapitated to disintegrate inside of me.

Lyme attacks your nervous system and manifests in a multitude of ways. For me, the symptoms from the first contraction arrived over a period of four years, scattered and spread out.

By 2004 I developed insomnia, which I simply used to my advantage. I lived in Montreal at the time, in a small studio apartment in the McGill ghetto where I was attending University. I rented the place for cheap not realizing I was the only person in the building under seventy-five. Old ladies liked to ask me to go to the corner dépanneur to buy them ketchup and sardines. My bookshelves were made out of bricks and wood from my cousins' garage. My cheap mattress – which lay on the tile – had been the floor model at the 'We sell everything but nothing you really want' store on Cote-St. Luc Road. I covered my walls with giant rolls of white paper and spent the long nights composing music upon them in an array of sharpie markers.

The same infomercials played over and over every night on the one channel I got on the 1970s TV I snatched from someone's trash; the first was for a very tall ladder, the second was for a very long paint roller which nullified the need for the very tall ladder, the third was for Ashley Madison, a match-making service that targeted married people looking to cheat on their spouses. I read textbook after textbook while I listened.

Some days I would go to class to take a midterm or final after two or three days of not sleeping. I'd come back from the exam and pass out. I'd wake up hours later with a vague memory of being at school. I'd laugh at the ideas that would suddenly appear in my head, like an essay thesis where I'd cited Kurt Vonnegut's call for extra U.S. Constitutional amendments as nonchalantly as I'd cited Alexis De Tocqueville and John Stuart Mill. I'd have flashbacks of an exam where I'd contrasted the philosophies of Rousseau and Hobbes by exhaustively comparing a real egg to a Cadbury egg. I'd wonder if I'd actually gone to class and written the exams using such essay topics or if I had just dreamed it all up. Turns out they were all quite real. Somehow I still walked away with A's.

The exams I do remember were filled with very serious people. Girls would close their eyes and cross themselves; guys would bounce their legs. I'd get looks from my fellow students, wondering why I was laughing, why I was so calm, found it all so amusing. People thought I smoked weed. Thought I was high. I wasn't. I was just so sleep deprived I wasn't really sure if I was awake. And it didn't much bother me at all.

I would have never put it together.
I would have never traced it back.

I soon developed tendinitis and the beginnings of arthritis. The doctors told me they believed it was from playing instruments my whole life too much, too hard. At one point, while working in a grocery store deli for rent money, cutting vegetables, my hands just cramped up. My right hand froze, so painful and swollen, that I was sent to the emergency room at the nearest hospital. The doctors put me in a cast for two weeks to force my hand to rest, even though they found no broken bones.

I took care of these joint problems on an as to need to basis. I carried hand warmers with me, the kind used by people who enjoy skiing and other below fifty-degree outdoor activities. I would heat up my hands before a show so they didn't cramp while playing keyboards or guitar. Once I forgot to throw the warmers out and quickly stuck them in my pockets when I got on stage. Halfway through the set I couldn't figure out why my legs were sweating profusely and it felt like my pants were on fire.

The doctors gave me little pink and purple squeeze balls with logos of various asthma medications printed on them so I could build up the strength in my fingers.

I would have never put it together.
I would have never traced it back.

Even after the rare nights where I got a real eight hours of sleep, I was usually exhausted. I started taking over the counter caffeine pills to get me up, and sweet vanilla Tylenol p.m. or lemon Theraflu tea to get me to sleep. The fatigue didn't take over my life completely but by 2004 it had revealed itself in many parts of me. It didn't matter whether I boxed endlessly with the heavy bag I hung in the corner of my apartment or walked up Mount Royal to the tams, my body always felt off, slow, my blood pressure's systolic number always sat way under 100.

I once tried to donate blood with friends at a school sponsored drive. For nearly thirty minutes the kind Jamaican nurse's gaze became increasingly impatient as it alternated between me, the clock, and my blood which moved through the tube with the urgency of a tortoise on muscle relaxers. She finally gave up on waiting for my body to pump out a sufficient donation, undid my line, and helped me up. I was awkwardly welcomed to an unmerited complimentary granola bar.

There were plenty of things I should have paid attention to, but I wasn't wired that way. When it came to thought, to another person's actions or emotions, I was the ultimate extractor. I was a super analyst of the most exhaustive degree. I gave more thought to discovering the emotional origins of why someone shifted their eyes a certain way or signed off a letter or email with "yours" or "love always" instead of "from," than I ever gave to discovering the origins of the problems of my body.

But when I began gaining weight, I decided that was it… I had finally had enough. I was going to see a doctor and I was going to lie through my freaking teeth to fix it as quickly as possible.

I easily bullshitted my way into getting a prescription for Adderall XR an A.D.H.D. drug. I didn't have Attention Deficit Hyperactivity Disorder but I had researched the unintended side effects of the drug and decided it was my best chance to get off the weight after all the normal routes I took had failed. Let's be honest, for those of you who don't know about Adderall, it is pretty much the prescription version of speed. If it makes it any better, I never took more than prescribed nor crushed up the pills between my teeth. I never snorted them up my nose like my classmates. Most of the time I felt very little effects of the drug on my mind at all, but it changed my body drastically. My blood pressure became normal again, my weight went down, my heart rate went up. The band-aids were working so why dig deeper? That wasn't my job… my job was to do what I had to do to keep moving forward. I had shit to do.

I would have never put it together.
I would have never traced it back.

I had always viewed my body as a nuisance and I treated its complaints as such. My body was a separate entity from me, one that had constantly gotten in the way of my life. It was the weight hanging around my invisible neck.

This disconnect wasn't helped by the fact that I entered the entertainment business at a young age, a business that's completely focused on ripping apart your looks. I was once called into a business meeting with a Grammy award winning production team who broke it down to me quite clearly. "You have the songs, you have the talent, you have the voice, you have a great look" they explained after talking to me for an hour about how much they loved my demo, "but you're not heroin chic and thin just doesn't sell. You should work on that and then give us a call again."

I was also told at that meeting that I should always tell people I'm twenty-one. So if you happened to wonder how old I am during this story… the answer's always twenty-one.

If I could've gone on without my body, I would have.

Perhaps if I had been more in tune with myself, if for once my body and mind were entwined rather than neighbors feuding over the dog shit on their lawns, maybe I would have taken these health issues more seriously; but I steamrolled past them with my eyes on the prize: a record deal, a college degree, earning enough money and status to have an impact on this world, enough to get my mom the life she deserves.

Playing with my band at the Peach Pit After Dark used to be top on that list but then I realized I was watching reruns… and it was fictional.

I burned the candle at both ends and smeared the burnt wax and ash across my face like war paint. I misconstrued my health problems as proof, battle scars earned from giving everything I had towards my future while surviving my past. I never thought those wounds were symptoms - the thought never even crossed my mind.

The day I pulled that tick off of me in the shower I knew something was terribly wrong, irretrievable, but I only allowed myself to feel that way for a second. With sensitive skin, I chalked up the circular rash to a normal reaction to any bug bite like a mosquito or spider.

I told my mom and my Aunt Carole about the rash to see if they thought anything of it, they didn't. Lyme disease was something dogs could get; that was the extent of what I knew, what my family knew. Being raised in the suburbs of San Diego, California, I never even heard of a human contracting it, let alone what would happen if one did.

Truth be told, there is no pamphlet on Lyme disease, no synopsis about it on the Internet that could have shown me even a peak into the true depths of its effects. There is nothing out there that could have prepared me for the absolute destruction that would follow its path.

There is an episode from *Roseanne* called "Toto We're Not in Kansas Anymore" where a tornado hits the fictional town of Lanford, Illinois. The extent of damage to the Conner's home is a shattered window and Roseanne's husband Dan's old underwear landing in a neighbor's tree, but Roseanne believes it was more than just a close call.

She tells Dan, "That tornado was a sign. A really big sign, more like a poster, no, more like a billboard, and it says in big letters…"

"What?" Dan interrupts her, "Repent, the end is near?"

"No," Roseanne responds. "It says 'sorry we missed you, will call again for another appointment', and it's signed the Tornado Man."

That first tick was my warning. It had only shattered my window, thrown some of my belongings off course, but it was coming back to get me, all of me. I just didn't know when.

3 oooh…. sooo… that's what i ordered?

The smack of my boots echoed throughout the cement stairwell as I ran from the last class of my spring semester and out the doors of Hamilton Hall to be greeted by a crisp whiff of New York City air. I made my way quick through the great gates on Broadway at 116th and slipped with a crowd underground onto the 1 train heading downtown.

I had transferred to Columbia University as a second semester sophomore from McGill. The final goal was always to go to Columbia University, more specifically, to study under renowned Historian and Political Scientist, Professor Manning Marable.

I worked three jobs, got myself on the Dean's list. I double majored in African American Studies and Political Science, working under Dr. Marable at the Center for Contemporary Black History. Through Dr. Marable I began working at the Doe Fund and was just starting to teach at Riker's Prison. I practically lived in I.R.A.A.S. (The Institute for Research in African American Studies) – I hardly ever went anywhere else on campus. I'd make a terrible tour guide.

It would take another book entirely to explain how gratifying and important it was to finally study under such extraordinary professors like Dr. Marable, Dr. Frederick

Harris and Dr. Farah Griffin and to finally be challenged and refined through their work. I had been looking for them my whole life and I was incredibly grateful to have finally found my home.

The other side of my world was music. There was a purpose to both sides. There was always a plan.

I jumped on the cross-town bus from Columbus Circle to the other end of Central Park stepping off to be greeted by one of my favorite city sights, the big bright grin of Sara, one of my closest friends in the world. Sara and I had been friends since I was in high school. We met while I was visiting my best friend in Boston. Sara was my first New York City roommate, my middle of the night caller, my insomniac confidant. She was my partner in gorilla marketing; passing out CDs with me outside of concerts, stickering light posts and piss-stink pay-phones in Alphabet City. We were a unique team, both pale skin and long red hair. Her eyes were a stunning light green, unlike mine of bright blue. Sara was an opera singer; promising, luminous, talented. Hard to miss.

 "Let's go!" She insisted still smiling, after a long hug and two liberal kisses on each cheek.

We rushed up the street towards a giant crowd exiting an outdoor concert. I kept a calendar of shows in the city to pass my music out at. I snuck into hundreds of venues, made my way backstage wherever I could to get my music to anyone who would take it. Every once in a while I'd sneak into the wrong door but see where it took me anyway. I once found myself watching a Tori Amos concert from thirty feet above her piano where I'd climbed onto the lighting rafters.

Word was spreading little by little and the calls were starting to come in.

By that spring of 2006, I had already met with the vice president of Virgin and Sony, as well as a number of production teams in Los Angeles and New York City. I was nominated as Best Female Artist and Best Rock Artist at the Toronto Independent Music Awards and had been invited by Randy Jackson to his recording studio after he listened to the demo I handed him in a fenced off V.I.P. lounge I snuck into at a Joan Jett concert.

I was being written up in independent magazines and was giving online and phone interviews. Some were extremely complimentary, some were awful, but press was noise and noise was good. The best compliment I got was from a major magazine who described me as - what would happen if Thom Yorke of Radiohead and P.J. Harvey were together long enough to have a love child. That was a very good day.

I handed Sara a stack of CDs from my backpack along with flyers for some upcoming shows. We went to work.

As the crowds finally began to dissipate back into the city with art and propaganda in hand, Sara and I made our way to a park bench for a breather. Sara slapped a fresh pack of American Spirits with her palm and unwrapped them as she stared at the band flyer.

"I can't believe you're finally going to play live out here!" She said, balancing her smile with lighting the cigarette hanging leisurely off the side of her mouth.

"Not much of a choice I guess…" I smiled. "Every suit I've met with has asked me to play live so they can get the *whole* picture."

"You should just get one of those one-man band setups! You could play piano with your feet and oh! You could have one of those hats that moonlights as a tambourine!"

For years I played every instrument on my recordings, except for some of the drums, so playing live had been the most difficult part of promoting my work.

"Where was this Mary Poppins insight before I invited my old bandmates to come out here?"

"How is it going with the band?" Sara asked sincerely.

"I have no idea what I was thinking," I shook my head.

"You were thinking it would be romantic!"

"And it was!" I laughed. "Childhood friends, high school bandmates, back together again! It was a really fucking romantic idea!"

"And?" She baited me.

"And?" I thought about it for a moment. "…You know the saying 'ask and you shall receive'?"

Sara nodded.

"They probably should've added: BE SPECIFIC."

The higher I was starting to get in music, the more apparent became the space inside me where joy was supposed to be. In an overtaking moment of nostalgia, I had emailed my former bandmates from high school asking them to form the new live band. Apparently it was a pretty convincing email because Jen, my violist, and Eric, my bassist, packed their bags, quit their jobs, left their friends and families and flew three thousand miles away from California and in with me.

"I still can't believe you had them move in with you," Sara said.

"What can I say?" I retorted. "I was thinking about how Kelly and Donna started that clothing boutique together, *Now Wear This*… brilliant name for a store by the way… and I thought about how Dylan and David and even Steve got behind the shop and helped them launch the Donna Martin Originals website? And I just thought, you know, I don't want to work this fucking hard for my dreams just to end up out there all by myself!"

"So you based another huge life-changing decision off of *Beverly Hills 90210*…"

I took the cigarette from between Sara's fingers and paused with a slow drag before I answered dryly.

"Yeah, that's about right."

We laughed.

"Are they at least paying rent?" Sara asked, dreading the answer, knowing me well.

I shook my head. I couldn't even look her in the eye.

"What?! What does your roommate say?"

"Oh shit! Did I forget to tell you about Mekia? She's had a pretty *engaging* summer," I filled Sara in using extremely excessive air quotes. "And by *engaging* summer, I mean, she is actually *engaged*. She's engaged to Peter."

"Are you serious?"

"Oh and pregnant. Did I forget to mention pregnant?"

Sara needed a moment.

"So let me get this straight, Jen moved into your bedroom with you, Eric is in a makeshift room off the kitchen, Mekia is engaged and pregnant, Peter is moving in? Which means you will have five, excuse me, five and a half people living in a two bedroom campus apartment?"

"Illegally," I corrected her.

"Of course illegally," Sara said taking another drag.

"So this is going to end wonderfully, eh?"

She was picking up my Canadian accent more and more those days.

"Oh yeah…" I smiled. "It's going to be amazing."

4 july 4th, 2006

I got up early to study for my summer school classes at one of my favorite libraries, the multileveled basement across from my apartment at the School of International and Public Affairs. I was hoping to get a jump-start on credits for the next semester. I reemerged to the humid afternoon air, hoping for a second wind. Missed call from my mom, missed voice-mail. I listened as I entered my building on 118th and climbed the three flights of stairs to my door.

"Hey baby girl, it's mom. I'm driving to work right now… probably shouldn't be on the phone, this guy is honking at me. Hold on. I'm going to let him pass and then honk at him."

I lifted my phone from my ear as the honking ensued. She continued, "I am so excited to hear about your work and school! Things on this end… well… I didn't know if I should tell you, but I got denied my request for a raise again. No raise in six years… I should quit. I'm so embarrassed. No, no, I'm lucky to have a job, even if it's with McDonald's," she tried convincing herself and then suddenly began to sing her words to the tune of *Joseph and the Amazing Technicolor Dream Coat*, "So give me a call back, my multicolored coat! My amazing…. Colored… *Oh shit there's a cop, gotta go.*"

I put down the phone and walked past Mekia and Peter's room then past the once spotless kitchen to find Eric's makeshift door partly open. Clothes and empty forties fell into the kitchen, covering the floor. His alarm clock was going off but he could've been in a coma for all I knew. The place smelled like alcohol and excessive sleep.

I opened my bedroom door to find Jen warming up on her viola.

"How was the library?"

"Peaceful," I sat down on my bed. "You think Eric's getting up for practice today?"

Jen half smiled and shrugged.

"Well," I checked my phone, "We got forty-five minutes till we have to be at the rehearsal studio to meet Eddie and Blue. I say we give him ten and then this time just go either way."

I packed up my telecaster, gig bag, pedals and chords and laced up my black and white chucks under my favorite pair of chocolate brown skinny jeans. I switched into a vintage grey Dylan McKay t-shirt, and grabbed my corduroy bomber jacket. I believed in always having one piece of sarcastic clothing on me at all times, if only to entertain myself. Accessories worked too.

The incessant beeping from Eric's alarm clock began again only to be silenced as it crashed into our shared wall. A moment later he arrived haggard in our doorway in a pair of pajama pants and a black Pantera t-shirt. He had a shaved head, auburn goatee, and brown eyes I remembered were once endlessly kind.

"What's the plan?" He asked, already agitated.

"We're leaving for the practice space in five... cool?" I asked. He walked away without saying a word.

"COOL?!" I yelled out to the other room.

Nothing.

Jen half smiled and shrugged again. I tried to laugh it off, but it was taking a toll.

The three of us made our way to 116th and Broadway, lugging our equipment onto the subway and down to a tall sleek building on thirty-eighth street. We had a battle of the bands competition coming up in four weeks on the Lower East Side, and another show at a club in Brooklyn in five. We arrived at the studio where Eddie, our drummer was twirling his drum sticks quietly next to Blue who was holding a wonderfully beat up chipped Stratocaster he could still make sound amazing. Both had been in the band about a month. Eric and Eddie walked down the hall ahead of us. Any tension I carried from Eric evaporated for a moment when I saw Blue smile.

"Hi Blue, long time no see," Jen said smirking,

"Very funny Jennifer," Blue answered as she passed to get the keys for the practice room.

Blue and I immediately regressed to children when we saw each other. We always tried to push each other over, pull each other's hair. Blue towered sixteen inches over me at six foot eight. He had an adoring Huck Finn quality about him, lanky with shaggy light brown hair and the soft blue eyes of a boy inflicted with a life-long case of wanderlust. He's the only person I ever met who dreamt of walking across the country as much as I did.

Blue pressed his palm against my forehead, holding me back as I attempted to throw loose punches at his stomach… my arms never reached.

"You ready to ROCK!?" He yelled jokingly.

"Fuck yeah I'm ready!" I yelled back. "Are YOU ready?"

Jen waived the key at us from down the hall. I remembered I was supposed to be in charge again.

The practice space was ambient, full of twinkling lights and an enormous mirror that covered one main wall of the windowless room. Eric sat in the corner twiddling with his bass.

We'd been rehearsing for nearly a month but Eric had yet to memorize even three of the songs. He didn't like to "work" on music… he just wanted to "feel" it. I would ask if he could *feel* himself learning the songs before we went on stage? Or *feel* himself getting his bass fixed, finding an amp to use before a show, getting to practice on time, helping me distribute flyers or work on the website? He didn't. I should never have offered him to come out there and he should never have accepted; he should have stayed in San Diego "feeling" other people's coffee at Starbucks.

"Any chance you're going to join the rest of us?" I asked.

His attitude was turning into a stridulous buzzing sound that was slowly becoming the only thing I could hear.

"I'm sitting right here," he answered.

"Yes, you're sitting. Notice anything odd about that, like the rest of us are standing? Except Eddie," I corrected myself. "But that's in his job description."

"So?"

"So the rest of us are trying to practice for a fucking show, that's what this giant obnoxious mirror is doing in here…"

Eric didn't move. I looked at Blue who mouthed 'Fuck it' and grinned.

I took a deep breath and nodded at Eddie to count us off again.

I hated that in order to play music I had to be on other peoples' asses to make sure everything I worked for didn't go down the can. I knew what I wanted, a quality not every-one was a fan of, but I was anything but green. I was on the radio for the first time at ten. I started my own production company with my older brother Stephen while in junior high and produced a number of large scale shows includ-ing a 2 act 14 song musical I co-wrote with him when I was twelve. By fourteen I released my first album. At fifteen I had two songs on the World Cup Soundtrack for the Winter Olympics. At seventeen my second album got me a spot as Jewel's featured artist on her website, my first taste of career irony since I absolutely can't stand Jewel.

I had been called controlling. I had been called bossy. But as Roseanne Conner once asked, "Is a farmer who turns a pig into a glazed ham bossy?"

Rehearsal ended and we gathered outside with our equipment, Eric and Eddie lit their cigarettes.

"What's the plan tonight? Want to come with me to meet some friends at the pier for fireworks?" Jen asked.

"I think I need to just take it easy, take advantage of Mekia and Peter being in Princeton for the night. Have fun though." I said quietly.

"Happy fourth everyone, I'm out" Eric announced, then clearly directed his gaze at me, "see you later *boss*."

He dialed his phone and walked up the street alone.

"And that's it for me ladies and gentleman," I declared throwing my hands up in a facetious acceptance of praise and surrender.

I gave everyone a hug and began walking the opposite way. Blue jogged to catch up with me.

"You okay?" He asked giving me a tighter hug.

"I don't know, I'm burnt... maybe if I go home, get some sleep..."

"What the hell is wrong with Eric? Did he just find out he got adopted or something?"

I laughed.

"I don't know, maybe he just got his period. I did find some tampons on his floor the other day... I should really pick him up a pamphlet or something."

Blue placed his hand in mine.

"I'll call you tonight?" He asked.

I smiled. We kissed each other on the cheek and silently went our separate ways on the block. I got to the corner and put my hands in my jacket pockets. I checked my jean pockets. I checked my backpack. I checked my gig bag, my guitar cases... I didn't have the keys to my apartment. I had lent them to Jen who was already on her way down to the pier. Eric had my spare. I had locked myself out.

The phone rang.
Sara was crying, she asked me to meet her.

Sara and I sat across from each other at a small table in an overpriced hole in the wall vegan restaurant in the East Village. The menu was full of bad new-age puns like "Peace and Carrots Casserole" and "Karma Kabobs."
"We're going to share the Random Acts of Hummus Kindness," I mumbled in humiliation to the waitress.
"What did you say?" She asked.
"Can we just have some hummus please?"

Sara's eyes were puffy and red. I hated seeing her sad. When she was having a hard day I would pick her up some awful pink-sugar covered marshmallow peeps or a bootleg two-dollar framed photo of *The Breakfast Club* I bought on the side of the street. When she got her wisdom teeth out I took the bus all the way across town with a heavy DVD player in hand and the newly released season 2 DVD set of *The Cosby Show* in my bag. We shared her painkillers and watched all night. We used to laugh so hard that some nights we would find messages from her roommate taped up on the bathroom mirror in the morning telling us to shut the fuck up. We laughed till we cried and vice versa.

"What's going on?" I asked softly.

"It's Blue." She answered.

I broke eye contact and reached for my wallet where I found my second Adderall of the day and swallowed it with a sip of water. I felt so tired.

"But what about Andrew? I thought that was going well," I hoped.

"But he's not Blue," Sara took a deep breath. "Just… just tell me we're going to end up together. Tell me that we're meant to be."

She had asked me these same questions so many times. I had met Blue through Sara back in Boston when I had visited in high school. They had been together off and on for five years. I hated to see her in pain but I also couldn't lie. I told her I thought she was incredibly beautiful and smart and talented. I told her that I knew she'd find someone that she could spend her life with, someone amazing.

Sara took my hands from across the table and asked me to please come back to her place, to the Fourth of July party at her building I had already declined.

I can't begin to tell you how many nights I spend dreaming about that single moment of my life.

Sometimes I dream I went home, back to my end of town, the unspoken edge of the city where yellow taxis stop and unmarked black cabs begin. Sometimes I dream I spent my night in the middle of an empty Columbia campus, lying on the center of the compass between the Low and Butler libraries, staring up at the few stars I could catch beyond the city lights. Sometimes I dream I went home and waited for my roommates on the cold cement bench across the street from my apartment outside the School of International and Public Affairs. Sometimes I dream I met Jen down at the pier, closed my eyes and listened to the fireworks. Other nights I dream I found solace walking through the hallowed Cathedral grounds of St. John the Divine.

In every dream, I always say no.

But I got on that train to Brooklyn - With Sara, back to Brooklyn.

Sara's loft was settled in the midst of a broken old warehouse in Williamsburg with its shattered windows that acted as home to thousands of diseased pigeons. The party moved freely between the roof of the building and the inside of the loft where drinks flowed freely. I sat alone at the back of the loft by the window – sober – marinating in disappointing thoughts about band practice earlier that day.

The day I met Sara in Boston, I had followed my best friend up a richly carpeted staircase that led to their fourth floor apartment at the corner of Gainsborough Drive. As we opened the door I heard my own voice coming out of speakers at the end of the narrow hall. Sara didn't know we were there and was singing loudly along to my music in her room. With blushed cheeks she introduced herself. She was embarrassed. I was flattered.

When someone knows you first through art there is no introductory phase. Many people I met believed they already knew me. They confided in me – immediately, they trusted me. They tended to ask my advice and take that advice much too seriously. There is a great deal of intimacy achieved very quickly, probably too quickly. With Sara, those lines of intimacy between us were blurred at best.

Sara had become the girl I trusted to get closer to than maybe anyone I'd ever had. She was the first non-relative I ever put down as my emergency contact when I went to the doctor or signed my lease. Sometimes, late at night, I would lay my head on her lap when we took the subway - she would stroke my hair or hold my hand… affection I wasn't used to. I felt safe when I slept next to her as I often did. She would tell me her secrets like many had before but surprisingly, I told her mine.

I watched as Sara worked the room slightly intoxicated, that big grin, the flirtatious body language. She could've had pretty much anyone there.

Blue arrived, suddenly stumbling through the front door with a small group of guys. I watched as Sara immediately flooded him with attention. He wasn't having it. He pushed past her as he spotted me.

"You're here!" He exclaimed grabbing me. We fell onto the couch as he pulled me down. "I didn't think you were going to be here but you're here!"

I tried haphazardly to push him off, feeling his whiskey breath and unshaven face brush against my cheek. Even drunk he was beautiful.

I could feel Sara watching us. She always watched but she could never see.

Blue grabbed my hand, "Come on, let's go. I'm going, we're going, let's go."

I couldn't.

Blue looked back at Sara and in frustration stood up from the love-seat.

"Goodnight Blue."

"Fine. I'll call you tomorrow."

I watched him leave and felt sick. Sara rushed over to the now empty seat next to me.

"Did he say anything about me?" She asked obliviously.

"No." I answered. "Sorry... I need a drink."

I grabbed a bottle of beer and found a seat on the plush green torn love-seat in the corner. I watched Sara mix back into the party. I was alone on a love-seat again, I was pathetic.

I had found myself in the middle of the bisexual version of the Brenda - Kelly - Dylan triangle from hell.

I wasn't even sure how I'd gotten there. Blue and I became friends while he and Sara were monogamous back when I first got to New York. We had a kinship that was completely separate from anything either of us had with her. He was one of the only musicians I knew who could leave me speechless when he sang. When he cheated on Sara months before they broke up, he called me at three in the morning to apologize. She called ten minutes later hysterical. When I asked him why he felt the need to not only confess, but apologize to *me* for his infidelity, he told me he didn't want me to think less of him, he didn't want to disappoint me.

I kept my mouth shut about the things Blue had begun to tell me in private. Sara didn't know that he too was calling me in the middle of the night when he couldn't sleep. That he didn't see the future with her that she saw. One late night of him crashing with me after practice turned into a string of nights that past month. We slept with our arms wrapped around each other in my bed. Those nights had turned into him telling me he was falling for me, and me telling him that I was falling for him too.

My guilt was relentless, but my actions were still. Everything between Blue and I had stayed physically fairly innocent. I let nothing happen and was beginning to hate Sara for it. I hated that I loved her as much as I did. I hated that while she ran around dating whomever she felt like, she never even considered that I could be competition to her. That the mere possibility that Blue, this beautiful boy, would want me, was never even a passing thought.

Or maybe she just didn't consider it because she trusted

me. Trusted I was her best friend. I still don't know which reason it was. I still don't know which reason is worse.

All I knew, sitting alone on that love-seat was that I couldn't be this person anymore. I was stuck between losing one of my best friends or an incredible rare chance at love. Either way I failed, I thought. Those thoughts turned into acknowledging my failure with my band, how badly practice had gone that morning how hard things were at home which was breaking my heart. Thinking about the band quickly snowballed into thoughts about my failures at life as a whole. I wasn't climbing fast enough. I wasn't helping my mom enough… I was failing her. Who I was no longer worked in my favor. Who I was had not produced the results I had wanted. You see, no matter how busy you keep yourself, no matter how hard you try, true loneliness finds a way of catching up to you; especially when you are fighting against it most. And that night I was fighting with everything I had left– but I could feel it… it had finally caught me.

I watched as Sara's roommates took out a baggy of weed and set it on the kitchen table. I had never smoked pot and I never planned to. I was a rarity in any place but a true oddity growing up in a beach town of Southern California.

I took a seat.

The bong had a sculpted glass frog on it. It is one of the last things I remember thinking before I inhaled. Frogs were always a symbol of bad luck in my life, like the plagues during a Passover Seder; I dipped my finger in the cup of wine. I watched Sara smoke, then her roommate, then her roommate's boyfriend. I had been at these types of tables since Jr. High School when my friends began snorting crystal meth off their desks in the back of class. Sometimes it was pot going around, sometimes cocaine; I was never offered out of respect. People were always quite clear on where I stood without me ever having to say a word.

Sara's roommate's boyfriend didn't know me well enough to know not to hand the bong to me in the first place, and I liked that. I liked that he had no expectations of me. I suddenly had no past to live up to, no high moral ground to walk alone upon.

When Sara looked the other way I took a hit... and as she looked back I saw the startled state of disbelief wash over her face as I let the smoke slip slowly out from between my lips. She knew me well. She knew I had made a mistake. I loved that look at first, the fact that I could surprise her, that I wasn't who she thought I was. I looked at her with a calm antipathy and without saying a word, brought the glass up to my mouth once more. Without moving my eyes from hers I took one more hit to drill my point home... I breathed in deep...

And then could not breath at all.

In a confusing state of loud coughs and vague laughs coming from her roommates at the table behind me. Sara watched as I got myself to the bathroom. My eyes in the mirror above the sink, so full of sadness, were the last thing I saw before I hit the floor.

"Shit! Sara! I don't think she's breathing!"
"What do we do?"

Muffled voices shouted out around me as I gasped, feeling air return finally to my lungs. I came to with everyone standing over me, my heart pounding so hard I could not speak.

I had stopped breathing, blacked out and collapsed on the floor in the hallway outside the bathroom. I looked down, my clothes were dripping. I had sweat through everything. I twisted my shirt and watched as the sweat fell onto my soaked legs. I looked up at Sara – I didn't know this kind of vulnerability could exist. There was a fight in my chest between my heart trying to run out of my body and my muscles trying to pull it back in.

"You're okay honey, you're okay," Sara kept repeating.
"Oh my g-d she's completely drenched," someone muttered above me.

Hardly breathing, I finally, uneasily, formed few words: Something is wrong. I'm on medication, I need help.

With all our past laying out in front of us, all we were and had ever been to each other in the balance, I watched, eyes blurred, as Sara started to run to the other side of the loft. I thought she was getting the phone to call for help...

Sara returned with a fan, faced it towards me, and turned it on.

I spent the next six hours getting out words when I could catch my breath and ignore the obscene pounding of my heart shocking every vessel in my body. With a steady air blowing in my face, I heard the fireworks explode outside Williamsburg and the cheers begin to rise. My heart beat the wind out of me, relentless. No heart is meant to work that hard to beat. I told her there was a drug-interaction taking place. I told her to call the paramedics. She didn't.

Maybe she was afraid to get caught with weed. Maybe there was coke at the apartment. Maybe she didn't think I was in as serious trouble as I was. Maybe the girl had bubbles in her think tank that night. But when it comes right down to it, I don't know if the why will ever matter.

Everyone went to sleep.

I sat in perfect stillness on the couch, waiting for my breath to come back to me. I waited six hours for my heart to stop beating the shit out of me. I waited six hours till I was able to see straight again. The whole room up until then had been a twitchy blur that shifted leaps and bounds each time I turned my head. When I could finally take a deep breath I scanned the empty loft. I became aware of everything that had just happened, I realized that everything was different now; there was no going back. There on the floor, I cried for the fear I hadn't had the capacity to express until that moment, I cried for the loss I knew had just taken place,

I cried until enough pressure was released from my body to allow it to move.

The sun was up. I was on the next subway out, before Sara even got out of bed.

I made it through that night but a part of me didn't. I did not get the help I needed but I did get the hell out of town to try and find it. I took a bus to Virginia. I took a bus to the unaired sequel to that episode of *Roseanne*... to the return of the Tornado-Man.

5 i could have walked to baltimore

My phone woke me up again. I rolled over in bed to see Jen reading Cosmo on the small black futon next to me.

"Sara again?" She asked.

"Yep… four missed calls already today," I answered checking my phone.

"What did the doctor say?"

"That you can't mix sixty milligrams of Adderall with weed. That it almost caused me to have a heart attack."

"You're on *sixty* milligrams of Adderall?"

"Not anymore."

My chest had killed for days. It still hurt to take a deep breath. I didn't know what to do about Sara. All I knew was I wanted space.

I was craving the quiet and mundane – some familiar suburban signs of life: A grocery store with aisles wider than a foot. A strip mall. Maybe a Taco Bell or Target. Parking lots.

There was a venue in Charlottesville that we had been offered to play at. Jen's old friends from college were playing a show there that night – it was the perfect excuse to get out of town. Jen and I grabbed our backpacks and took off to that old Blue Mountain state.

We took a Chinatown bus that smelled like stale urine

from N.Y.C. through Philadelphia and D.C. dropping us off in the outskirts of Baltimore. The bus left us on the side of the road next to a well-groomed lawn across the street from a fairly new looking McDonald's. One of Jen's friends was supposed to meet us there and drive us the rest of the way to Charlottesville.

"OOOH CAN YOU FEEL IT?!" I howled taking an exaggerated deep breath in.

I smiled – wide – at the fresh air, at the ability to see forty feet ahead of me without hitting another concrete wall. I don't think I had smiled for days.

"She's going to be late," Jen said, hanging up her cell phone annoyed.

"Great," I shrugged and smiled back sincerely, "let's walk to Baltimore!"

I could see the city in the distance, the tall gathering of steel and glass. I had traveled the country many times, but Baltimore was one place I'd never been.

"Are you joking?" She asked rhetorically.

She knew me well enough to know I wasn't

"Here," I took out a splitter for my iPod and gave her a pair of headphones connected to mine which I slid back over my ears.

"TO BALTIMORE!" I said still smiling like a child, pointing out into the distance. Walking tall.

I'm not sure when I had last been as excited as I was at

that moment. I wanted an adventure. I wanted to walk until I found answers. I wanted to walk until I found relief to heal my sore heart. I felt an immediate surge of liberation as The Decemberists' tinny steel strings of "Engine Driver" began; five short strums and switch… six more strums and switch. I lost myself in Colin's voice swooning in my ears, the violins mimicked the melody, walking up the scale behind the vocals slowly as Jen lagged behind me unconvinced.

"She shouldn't be long," Jen interrupted loudly over the music, I felt our connected headphones pull me back as they tugged off my ears. She had stopped walking. "Let's just wait here."

We were standing in front of an old red brick building. The words "Beer House" were stenciled in faded white paint over the door. Seriously? We were only six blocks in on our quest. I had no interest in sitting in a bar, we had just left the confines of New York City and the Chinese urine bus. I didn't want to sit still or merge my troubles with fermented barley and hops. I may have wanted to keep walking but things were so rough with Eric and the band back home I didn't want any more tension. If she wanted to wait there, I would.

I turned off the music and followed Jen quietly into the bar. I found a booth while she went to get a beer. The few older men sitting on wooden stools at the counter turned around to watch their unexpected company take a seat; these two young girls on their home turf.

I loved Jen even though we had absolutely nothing in

common but music. We had known each other since we were ten years old, she had been playing viola for me since we were about fifteen. On one hand, when Jen played music she transformed, she evoked something other worldly, she became a medium for some great message, some beautiful cry communicating through her fingers – her strings. She was classically trained. I played piano, bass, drums, guitar, and vocals, but I couldn't read a lick of music. When I wrote for her she had to listen carefully, understand the strange language of sound I heard in my head. She had been around me long enough to understand how I spoke. She understood how my hand gestures translated into timbre, vibrato, pizzicato. I looked to her as a musical puzzle solver, as a magic interpreter of sorts.

On the other hand, Jen liked to salsa dance.
I never knew how to respond to that.

Jen's speaking voice sounded as if it emanated solely from the roof of her mouth. She referred to herself as that one girl that's always on every season of MTV's *The Real World* - the one who agrees with everyone to his or her face, then retracts when behind their back. I was never sure how to respond to that either.

But with music, we were different people to each other. I was never the jam band type, I would venture to say this may actually be the first time I ever even used the word jam without talking about peanut butter. I didn't like to play with too many people. Music can be a very vulnerable place to bring someone into. In music I trusted Jen with the deepest parts of me, the most broken, the most brave. She had told me countless times that she attended Boston University to study music so that she could be a better violist for me, and now she had followed through, moving three thousand miles across the country to live and play music with me. Sometimes it felt like an honor. Sometimes it felt like another overwhelming responsibility.

Jen drank as she checked her phone for messages from her friend, each one still saying she'd be there soon. I stared out the window and watched the sun slowly go down over the congregating skyscrapers – turning them hour by hour into darker silhouettes of a place that now seemed so far out of reach.

"Our ride will be here soon," Jen told me, ordering another beer, flipping closed her cell phone again. Jen always smiled on only one side of her mouth. "I promise."

We sat for five and a half hours at that stinking booth, until the city completely disappeared into the fog drenched stars. We finally climbed into a lifted SUV, I sat in the back silently and listened as Jen's tiny mouse-like friend shouted at the little cars stuck in the traffic ahead of us. She and Jen went to college with the band that we were going to see play in Charlottesville. They were a group of guys I had met years earlier back in Boston. We arrived just in time to see the end of their set.

The music was shit – a rip off of the Dave Matthew's

band – which is torture if you, like me, want to stab yourself with a fork when you hear the *real* Dave Matthew's Band. The venue had promise though. I sat in the back of the room at an empty table, running through prospective set lists for us on a napkin.

We followed the band back to a farmhouse where they all lived and practiced. We drove miles and miles outside of what was already a small town. The further we followed the more I prayed we'd turn around.

"I thought they lived in Charlottesville?" I asked quietly from the back.

Jen and her mouse friend couldn't hear me, they were too busy torturing me by blasting the soundtrack of RENT. I considered jumping out of the car.

I watched as the cool dark, lit by the nearby university, faded to a deep and flawless black. Up through the mountains past paddocks and fields full of vague shadows of tired horses – up through the dark twisting trees, up a steep, winding and tight dirt road, we arrived at the top to find an old wooden farmhouse. The frogs screamed from the leech filled pond, the ghost white moths circled the porch light in a panic, waiting for heaven to arrive.

What the fuck am I doing here? I asked myself silently.

I had wanted the suburbs, I had wanted a break from the city but I didn't want this! I had turned into a repetitive T.S. Eliot poem, with the band, my love life, this trip. I was Alfred J. Prufrock and this was not what I'd meant at all, this was not it at all.

I paused at the porch with a complete uneasiness, there was no way out. I walked into the house and felt no relief as a hostile grasshopper the size of my hand jumped over my foot. Two stained and dirt covered pull out couches sat facing each other across the living room. Jen and her friend took one and began setting it up. Apparently the other one was mine.

I didn't want to be alone there but I was. Jen and her mouse friend went right to sleep.

I tried wiping off as much dirt from the sheets as I could and laid on my back staring at the black void that would eventually become the ceiling come daylight. I wanted to run, but I had no way to get out of there. I had no car and even if I stole someone's I had no idea how to get back to civilization. There weren't even paved roads anywhere near by. It was dead silent, minus the ceaseless chirping. I couldn't take it anymore.

I got up and found the knotted wooden railing of the staircase in the dark. I knew that Justin, the violinist for the band, would be upstairs. He and I had spent some time together in New York City. His door was partially open; the light slipped through the crack and dimly lit up the landing.

"Hey Ace, I can't sleep," I whispered to him through the doorway.

He invited me in.

"Not what you expected?" He asked.

I smiled. I noticed a bottle of painkillers on his dresser.

They would knock me out enough to get me through the night. It was either that or try to find my way through the woods to a Howard Johnson's. Plus, he owed me.

Years earlier he had once spent the night at my place with a group of friends. We had flirted all night. I was falling asleep, cuddling with him when out of nowhere another girl climbed onto the bed. Before I knew what was happening he had taken his arms off from around me and was on his back with this girl giving him a blow-job right next to me, right there on *my* fucking bed! I left and slept on the couch. He apologized profusely to me the next morning. Blamed it on the alcohol.

…Like I said, he owed me.

"Here, help yourself," he said handing me the bottle. He was recovering from a motorcycle accident and had plenty of pills to spare. I popped a few in my mouth and stuck a handful in my front pocket. I went back downstairs and waited for them to hit my head, till I could black out and embrace the miracle of fabricated peace. I took two more and put my headphones on, my iPod automatically shuffling songs to serenade the silence away. I passed out alone. I woke up with a farm dog curled up on top of me.

Something was very wrong.

"You smell like a bus," I mumbled to the dog, gently pushing him off of me. I went to wash my face. I looked down to find my arms and legs covered in rashes. Small itchy red hive-like marks that climbed down from my shoulders to my fingertips.

I went to the front porch where everyone was drinking coffee. I found Justin bent down over the dog, dissecting his fur.

"Shit," he said.

"What is it?" I asked him. Nobody else was paying any attention.

"Oh nothing," he said blindly, "he's just got a bunch of ticks crawling on him again."

Fuck.

I knew what I was feeling. I had only felt it once before. I remembered the field, the photograph, the shower... I could see the blood run down my stomach. Something was terribly wrong. Something was irreversible.

I had been bit.
Again.

It is somewhat of a rarity to contract Lyme disease once; I can't imagine how rare it is to contract it twice. Then again, I never did much half-assed.

I wanted to walk to Baltimore. I should have just done that instead.

6 the lonely girl and the bad grilled cheese

The rashes began to fade shortly after I returned to New York City. I didn't give myself time to stop and think. I never bothered to get the rashes checked. I was overly preoccupied with music, work, school, and the usual and unusual drama of friends and lovers. I had things to do! There was only so much summer left before the fall semester would begin. I was going to be a senior!

Rah rah siss boom bah.

Blue and I spent a string of nights together when I got back from Virginia. Jen slept in the living room and Blue and I would lay in my bed in next to nothing, falling asleep with his heavy arms around me. I would fall asleep to his constant breath, his legs hanging over the edge of my full size bed, his lips brushing against the back of my neck. An empty bottle of Kahlua and two dirty shot glasses were always scattered on the floor next to us, next to his clothes, where we had stomped our feet and played guitar all night, singing at the top of our lungs. We would fall asleep to that distinct smell of New York City, the mix of Northeast heat and slightly peeling lead paint, that filled the thick summer air.

Everything that had happened with Sara on July 4th should've made me feel free to pursue Blue, but I only felt more conflicted. It felt like we were all tied together even tighter than before and that made me feel sick.

Then one night, Blue told me he had an opportunity to move to Austin, to join a band with his best friend from childhood. I knew he had to go. We stayed up pondering the proverbial sunrise we believed was finally coming up for each of us. In the morning he was gone.

I found myself constantly coming down with what I believed was a flu that wouldn't quit. Jen entered our room tired from her first week as a hostess in mid-town. I had set her up with the job through my friends to help her make some extra cash. My dresser was covered in cold and flu medicine. My trash filled with used Kleenex. I was struggling to lace my shoes.

"Hey, I'm going to have a talk with Eric while you're gone," Jen said sincerely, taking a seat across from me. "I know he's not used to the pressure or working this hard but he shouldn't be taking it out on you, I just can't stand how he's been treating you. It's affecting the band as a whole."

"Wow…" She had caught me a bit off guard. "Thank you."

I was hopeful that we could all still make it work.

"I'm sorry to ditch you guys," I continued, "I just haven't seen my mom in forever and she's not a fan of the city."

"You sure you're well enough to go?" Jen asked.

"Yeah… I'll be alright. How long can I possibly have a fever for?"

I was run down. I had a constant sore throat. I was starting to get sick to my stomach. I thought maybe I had caught something from the cheap falafel stand in the West Village my friends and I frequented. Seriously.

You're probably thinking: For an Ivy League girl, you sound like an idiot.

Maybe.

It's hard not to think that when I look back too. But you have to remember, I was all-cerebral.

I wrote music in my dreams. I remembered nearly every word said to me. I had a form of hyperthymesia – hence this book.

The thing is, I could tell you stories of how I'd ended up the kind of person who would let not one but *two* ticks bite her without stopping long enough to wonder if it was worth looking into. I could explain how I had become the kind of person who would fall for someone only to write a song about it rather than *act*. I am very much aware of how I became a person who was so separated from her body that she could hardly feel a thing, but I'll give you the Reader's Digest version:

When I was a kid, separating from myself was a necessity. I had to become an observer. I had to observe and often laugh or create, in order to survive.

I was only four when a babysitter, a neighbor's seventeen-year-old son, tied me up and put a pillow over my head. He cornered me, tried to get me out of my pajamas. My parents came home in time to stop it – opening the front door only to watch as he ran down the stairs and past them out of the house pulling up his zipper. My father did nothing, didn't want to ruffle any feathers in our new neighborhood. My mom called the police who summoned us to the station to file a report. The police sent me to a doctor who gave me a full gynecological exam. If you're a girl reading this, you know that is an intrusive exam at any age, but it is life changing at the age of four.

Only a few years later I became aware of the psychological and verbal abuse I was witnessing being inflicted on my mother and older brother by my father on a daily basis. When you're seven years old and your father is calling your brother a faggot and a loser and your mother an idiot every time they turn around, there isn't much you can do but watch.

By the time I was in first grade I was such an observer that I had begun the habit of manipulating my tiny hands into the shape of an old 1900's video camera... I'd scan rooms with one eye closed, my right hand mimicking an invisible hand-crank, while I peered with my left eye through the small hole in my slightly open left fist.

Like most suburban households, the abuse and intimidation was limited to behind the closed identical door on our tracked home street. But sometimes, on vacations or outings, the truth was revealed.

One evening, all four of us were at Red Robin when my father lost it. He began screaming at my mom – calling her a whore. This was a strange term he used regularly, considering the only man she'd ever slept with was him. Then again, my mom once came home with a modest nightgown from Victoria Secret for their anniversary and he went on a rampage about what a slut she was. He got in her face often, he threw his fist through the drywall inches from her head.

While he screamed and onlookers watched unsure of what to do, I slipped down in the booth, under the table, and crawled out unnoticed. I found the waitress and pulled on her pant leg. I whispered in her ear as she leaned down to hear me. I snuck back into the booth next to my brother. My father was still going. Moments later, in the middle of my father cursing over the table at my mom, out came a giant slice of ice cream cake lit up with a single candle, surrounded by seven waiters and waitresses who gathered around the table clapping their hands and singing:

"Do we have a birthday here? Yes we have a birthday here! Birthday where? Birthday here! Hooray!!!"

My father was stunned into temporary silence as my tactic intended. My brother and I were cracking up.

The wait staff placed the huge slice of cake in front of my mother. I met her bloodshot eyes through the candle as she made her wish.

I didn't have to ask what it was.

I witnessed and was on the receiving end of further psychological and verbal abuses for years by my father and others. I dealt with an attempted suicide by a relative. I had been chased down flights of stairs, I had been physically threatened. I was told over and over that no one would ever love me.

I grew up naively jealous of oversimplified storylines I watched on *Beverly Hills, 90210* about Alcoholic parents. At least they had a parent whose abuses were based off of something external, I thought, something that could be removed. I wished the sickness I saw had a cure that simple.

I grew up envying the extraordinary honesty expressed on the episodes of *Roseanne* I cuddled up with every night. I envied the community they were a part of. The suburbs I grew up in were a place of secrets, of conspicuous consumption, and neighbors unknown. The only time I saw more than two of my neighbors on the street at a time was when a house across the street from us burst into flames. The suburbs are a strange place where many share a struggle but comradery is nearly non-existent.

I was eleven when I found out I was an illegal alien and was given strict instructions to make sure nobody in the very republican town we lived in found out. It turned out my father was not from Florida like he'd always told us. He was a full blooded Canadian like the rest of us and had started a large telemarketing business in Southern California under a fake social security number.

It was a strange to be the subject of debate and discrimination but lucky enough that nobody knew it. As a white kid, I was privy to the bigotry of our city, listened as my mom was encouraged by our neighbors to sign petitions to keep illegals from attending the public schools my brother and I were at. We once had the INS come pounding on our door. They told my mom they believed there was an illegal alien on the premises. Turns out they were talking about the gardener. I helped him hide as my mom kept them distracted.

By my teens, I found no relief. I spent almost all my time watching my mother lay in a hospital bed with cancer. I lost friends to jail and I lost friends to death. I attended 11 funerals by the time I was 18 years old, I spoke at 6 of them. Suicides, drug overdoses, car accidents, murder... the list goes on and on.

Let's just say, I saw a lot I shouldn't have seen, things nobody should have to see, and I learned how to disconnect.

I've heard some people disconnect from their body in order to avoid feeling pain. I don't think for someone like me that really covers it. I disconnected because feeling too much would get in my way, distract me from where I was going. I had no time to lose.

I actually learned to *pride* myself on ignoring my body. I not only prided myself, but I pushed the limits to see how far I could take it. I spent many winters in Montreal walking around with shorts and bare feet in zero degree weather. If people could train their minds to ignore hot coals, I could train mine to ignore the bitter cold.

I took my moderate insomnia and pushed it further,

avoiding sleep on purpose. I'd spend nights working on projects, like seeing if I could get through listening and reading along to the entire nineteen hour version of the new testament on tape as read by James Earl Jones.

My mind was the only thing I looked out for. Mind over matter. Mind over everything. Mind over common sense.

Luckily, I was a musician, a writer. I started playing piano at four and guitar at seven, I wrote my first song called, "We are Kings" with a large powder blue felt tip marker when I was five. Everything for me was material, everything was a candidate for alchemy and entertainment, even when it shouldn't have been.

I met my mom at JFK and she rented us a car to drive to Montreal for a few days with a detour through the Pocono's Mountains in Pennsylvania.

My mom is like nobody you've ever met, I can pretty much guarantee it. She got her B.A. in criminology but got two more degrees from night school after she became a single mother; one to become a teacher, another to become a veterinary nurse. She's been a preschool teacher, a horseback riding instructor, she worked the graveyard shift as a vet assistant at an emergency animal hospital when I was in high school, she lived in her RV at the stables to deliver foals in the middle of the night during spring, she has a dog-sitting business, competed in the rodeo, runs summer camps to teach kids about animals, works at seven McDonald's restaurants as a hospitality manager, volunteered with physical therapy at children's hospitals, sold leather cowboy belts she custom tooled to truck drivers, taught herself woodworking and built custom made-to-order coffins for a pet cemetery. The last was a little awkward to explain to friends.

My mom is the most adorable petite 5 foot 2 blonde haired blue-eyed woman; she resembles a young Betty White. Even though we lived in tracked housing and were part of a suburban homeowners association, she built a coral in the backyard and brought her horse home to visit and stay the night. She bought chickens and a miniature pygmy goat that walked freely in and out of our house, they sat on the couch with everyone else. My mom loves to rebel. She has a built in sixties radio in her head. When she dances she kicks her feet.

At around two in the morning, on the way to the motel, my mom and I came across a restaurant chain called Perkins. This Perkins had worse food than Denny's, and an ambiance too stale to compare to the white trash charm of a southern Waffle House. We sat at the third booth in on the right.

"I can't wait till one day I'm a senior," my mom prattled on while thumbing through the sticky menu the waitress had accidentally left at our table after taking our orders. "I'm going to eat dinner at five thirty every night – pot roast and mashed potatoes off the senior menus! Oh shoot… I wonder if they have hot dogs and beans here? I should have checked to see if they had hot dogs and beans."

The waitress brought out our food. My mom always travels with Omega, our sweet and stout little English yellow lab who was hiding under the table.

"You look run down," my mom commented.

"I'm alright…" I said, picking at my grilled cheese and feeding most of it to the dog. It was by far one of the worst grilled cheese sandwiches I've ever had in my life. Seriously, how do you fuck up a grilled cheese?

My mom had begun telling me a story about how she set up two eighty something year olds who both frequented McDonald's, when all of sudden, a group of ten girls in matching uniforms walked through the front door of Perkins.

One girl caught my attention. She was stunning.

As the group walked past us, the only girl I had noticed paused, turned around and walked back towards me. I couldn't believe it. She stopped in front of our booth interrupting my mom's story. She asked us about Omega who was sticking her face out under the table. She introduced herself.

Her name was Kayden.

Before I even got out my name, let alone an invitation, she sat down next to me on my side of the booth and began talking with my mom about service animals and California. I just stared. I was pretty sleep-deprived so I blankly stared at a lot of things, but this was different, I think I would have stared at her anyway.

I got caught in her light blue eyes, her soft features, the small freckles that fell around the corners of her mouth. After minutes of being completely tongue tied, I finally got up enough nerve to make my move. In the middle of her talking, I brushed away a part of her long light blonde hair and touched the diamond piercing on the inside of her right ear.

"I like this…" I said quietly touching the earring.

This was my extent of flirting. No joke. Try not to be intimidated by amazingness… I could totally be the next Mystery.

Sara used to sit with me and try to teach me how to flirt, she would briefly touch my leg or move the hair out of my eyes while we talked and then let me practice such subtleties back on her. I was hopeless.

It was irrefutably odd that Kayden was sitting with us. I watched as her identically dressed friends from the other side of the restaurant tried to wave her down with confused faces and exaggerated - aggravated gestures. She wouldn't get up.

They had been working as counselors at a summer camp together and had been drinking a bit that night, but I knew that wasn't why Kayden was being so bold. She was lonely. I could see it as soon as she walked through that door.

After about a half an hour of finding my tongue still

tied, I excused myself to the car so that I could execute the only other B.S. flirtatious move I knew:

I handed her a copy of my CD.

My music had a tendency to speak louder than I did. I'm always told my voice in person is much different than in my music. I'm never sure what people are expecting, for me to belt out pleasantries? I talk somewhat low, a little raspy, a little quiet - like I'm always subconsciously saving my voice to sing.

I can tell you on several occasions I've been lovingly compared to Brad Pitt in *Snatch*.

"Is this you?" She asked.
"I play music." I answered like a total moron.
She smiled.
"I can't wait to listen to it." She took the receipt from the table and turned it over. "Can I have your number? Or email? I'll let you know what I think."
I wrote down my contact info and put it in her hand.

Kayden and I hugged for the first time. I breathed in and closed my eyes as I felt her body press against me tightly. We fit perfectly. It was one of those hugs that lasted longer than it should have. For a moment I completely forgot everything that had been happening that summer. I walked back to the car, unable to wipe the lost smile off my face. My mom looked at me as she turned over the engine of the rental car.

~ the lonely girl and the bad grilled cheese ~

"I think she likes you," she said.

I didn't believe her. I should have.

7 confused summer runaway

I got back from my mini trip feeling somewhat renewed, a little part of me still basking in the glow of meeting a beautiful stranger. I entered the apartment and said hello to Peter and Mekia, who was increasingly showing. The two were hanging out in their room watching a movie. I walked past the kitchen and saw Eric wasn't home.

"Jennifer!" I yelled out thinking she was in our room, "I'm home! Sorry but I couldn't find you a wagon wheel from Amish country…"

I stopped, noticing a note smacked onto my door with duct tape.

SEE YOU IN VALHALLA! - ERIC

Sometimes I wish I were making this shit up. Apparently Eric was announcing his intent to not only continue battling me here on earth, but forever, in some kind of Viking warrior afterlife.

I ripped off the note and threw it onto the floor entering my room. My smile was gone. Eric and I used to have so much fun together. He used to laugh so loudly it was contagious. Eric and I used to do things like sneak into our old drummer's parents' kitchen when we were in high school and change the names of all the food in their pantry to dirty words by marking out letters on the labels with sharpie markers. I missed that guy. I lay down on my bed and closed my eyes.

I fell asleep.

I woke up gasping for air. Ever since the fourth I'd been having increasingly severe nightmares where I couldn't breathe. Sometimes I'd wake up in the middle of the night drenched in sweat. I would sneak out to the living room and turn on *Roseanne* on Nick at Nite to drown out the panic in my head.

I'd spend the night with my siblings: Darlene, D.J. and Becky; then sneak back into bed at dawn before Jen woke.

The nightmares always came back though. In this one I was laying at the bottom of swimming pool, an enormous grey elephant was standing with one of his giant legs on my chest as I screamed underwater at the top of my lungs. The elephant lifted his trunk in victory, ferociously trumpeting into the sky.

Laughter erupted in the living room outside my bedroom door; Jen and Eric were back. I opened the door to find them both wasted. Eric stared back at me as he took out a forty from a brown paper bag and made himself at home on my living room couch. He didn't say a word to me. Jen came into our room and closed the door behind us.

"What's going on?" I whispered.

"We went to play darts! How's your mom?" Jen answered.

"Fine Jen, what the hell is going on with Eric?"

"Oh who knows."

Jen began getting ready for bed.

"Well I thought *you* might know… how did it go?"

"How did what go?"

"Talking to Eric?" I asked, "about how he's been acting, how it's affecting the band? All that stuff… remember?"

"You know…" she said, flashing her trademark half-mouthed smile, "I decided to stay out of it, you know?

I wanted to throw her out the window.

"I just really don't want to pick a side," she continued, taking off her shoes and climbing into bed only three feet away from me.

I sat down and watched as Jen fell asleep intoxicated. I sat there for over an hour, thinking about how this was supposed to be *my* home, a safe place where I didn't have to be afraid of what was going to happen next. Somehow I ended up with someone who hated me living down the hall from me on my wallet, slamming doors on me, speaking coldly, living off my mistaken generosity. And now, here in my *bedroom*, for Christ sake, the only sanctuary I had left, was being shared with someone who when push came to shove, absolutely did not have my back.

I felt so incredibly used.

I remember thinking:
If they want to take it all, they can have it.

Around four a.m. I packed a few things and grabbed my backpack. I taped a note to the television saying, "rehearsal is canceled," and I left.

Now, I had *no* idea how sick I was at the time, but you know some of your wires are definitely getting crossed in your brain when you runaway from your own home.

In the low light of the morning meeting the all-night lights hitting the sky from the city, I went for a walk. I walked seventy-five blocks, from Harlem to a near empty Times Square where the billboards still flashed and flickered under the false impression that anyone was around to care. I took the subway to 14th street where I met a friend over breakfast at the three story Whole Foods in Union Square. I tried to eat but I couldn't keep anything down.

I followed my friend down to the Financial District; to a modern dance class she had at eight a.m.

I rolled up my hoodie as a pillow and lay down on the cold floor in the corner of the dance studio next to the large legs of a black grand piano. I watched the feet of a dozen dancers, pointing, searching, skipping in graceful unison across the floor. I dozed off. I opened my eyes to see a man in tights with curly brown hair looking over me.

"I heard that you play the piano," he said with a thick French accent. I looked around realizing there was a room of dancers staring at me. He was the choreographer.

"Yeah, yeah I do," I stammered pulling myself up quickly off the floor.

"You play something for us to dance to?" He insisted in the polite form of a question.

I squeezed my red eyes closed tight to make sure I wasn't dreaming. I was living in what felt like a perpetual hynopompic state, waiting for someone to fully wake me. I sat down at the hard wooden bench and played. I watched these people softly sway and spin in waves of sound that came from my fingertips. He raised his hands to stop, I heard applause, I smiled gently and got on the subway to the Upper East Side.

I arrived at 86th and First Avenue. I slept on a couch of another friend from California and watched *A League of Their Own* and *Fried Green Tomatoes*. I didn't leave her apartment for three days. I didn't even leave the couch. I strayed in and out of consciousness – sickness had followed me there. It was beginning to force me in and out of states of panic that now followed me out of dreams and into the light of day.

I tried to buy some food and realized I had negative four hundred and twenty six dollars in my bank account.

I didn't know what to do... so I decided to start walking again.

Starting again at 90th and 2nd Avenue, I walked in a daze for hours. I walked until I found the Williamsburg Bridge and then, I kept walking.

In the middle of the bridge, while the cars flew by and the water swirled under the spaces in the metal that pushed up against my tired feet, I listened to my voice-mail. I stood there, dead center of the bridge, listening to a message from Eric, screaming at me for canceling rehearsal. I laughed. Apparently he planned to go to rehearsal that day. He hadn't even noticed I had been gone for three days. I thought about throwing my phone over the bridge. I then thought for a brief moment about stepping up on that ledge myself and just letting go… giving myself permission to fall. I imagined the air rising up under me peacefully before the water washed it all away.

Somehow I kept walking.

I walked all the way to what would be the Montrose stop on the L line in Brooklyn. I fell asleep on a cement bench in a park, listening to the sound of skateboard trucks grind against the walls around me.

It was getting dark. I rang another friend's doorbell, had a glass of water, turned around, got on the subway and went home. I told Eric to get the fuck out of my house.

We had been friends for over 8 years.
I never saw him again.

This was a long first step into the lesson that all who are sick must eventually learn: when you are fighting an illness, when you are fighting yourself, you have no energy left to spend fighting anybody else. Anything that strains you more than serves you, anyone who stresses you more than eases you, must be severed.

Or as Donna Martin put it:
Scan. Discard. Select. Move on.

"Maybe I should go home to San Diego for awhile after we play the shows and before fall semester starts." I told Jen.

I believed a little time at home would make things better, time to decompress from all the drama with the band. Jen wanted to go home as well and see her boyfriend. We agreed that we would talk once we were in San Diego and decide what to do next. I was beginning to accept that whatever was happening to my body and slowly my brain was not going away. The states of panic, the flu symptoms, the exhaustion, I believed it was stress. All I needed was a break to get my head together at home. Plus, it was my mom's birthday, and I'd never missed it.

A couple weeks later I borrowed some cash and caught a plane back to San Diego.

I faded in and out of sleep on the bus to La Guardia Airport. I lost myself in the hundreds of passengers coming and going silently by while I clung tightly to my headphones under my hood. I listened to Sufjan Stevens' magnificently hypnotizing album *Illinois* as I entered the plane and took my seat. We departed with cruel mockery above the overcrowded Riker's prison near by.

We had barely nicked a dent in the boundary line of Eastern time when

...All hell broke loose.

8 the sun set upon the summer

I sat shaking in the back of the plane with the oxygen mask over my face. I could not turn around. I did not want to see the aisle, the seats, the people. I sat facing the back of the plane, in one of the tiny makeshift seats that pulled down from the wall for the flight attendants. I prayed my will would outweigh the speed of the plane and force us to fly backwards, to a time when I was well. I had to go back.

My eyes set upon the microwave oven, the tiny compartments full of miniature cans of sodas and small bags of blue chips. A flight attendant tried to distract me by telling me stories about his teenage daughters, checking the oxygen tank intermittently. He kept cool but had hardly left my side for over five hours. I had been talking to myself out loud in my seat, prior to throwing up twelve times in the tiny flying toilet in the sky. I threw up until I couldn't see straight, so hard that I thought I may have thrown up my soul which now lay submerged at the bottom of the dark thick blue water.

Then came the chest pains and the difficulty breathing. Then came the fainting and being pulled up off the floor by flight attendants... hence the oxygen.

I had been telling myself over and over to calm down as soon as the plane took off. I wanted out. I thought hearing my own voice out loud would help get me out of my head, somehow make me present, but it didn't work. The more I realized I was speaking out loud to myself, the crazier I started to think I was, and the more panicked I became. I tried concentrating on Sufjan calmly singing to me about stories of states I had once seen. But the antsiness came from inside my bones.

I couldn't stay in my seat.

I didn't want to be in the sky. I wanted the ground. I wanted to lay on the ground. I had to get out! 'I am trapped,' I thought, 'in a giant metal tin can!" I wanted them to land the plane. I wanted to jump. If I'd had a parachute I would've used all that was left of my strength to open that emergency door, push that metal handle down with all the weight of my being. I would feel all the air of the world come rushing in. The tiny soda cans would fly up and hit the roof of their mother ship. The cabin would be filled with floating blue chips circling the heads of screaming passengers. And I would jump.

And finally I would be free.

By the time I landed, I was no longer the same person. I opened my eyes and found myself in my backyard, sitting in the grass unable to speak. I was indescribably confused. I opened my eyes and found myself on the way to the emergency room. I locked the passenger door as we drove now suddenly afraid I would throw myself out in the middle of speeding traffic.

The funny thing is, even in the midst of confusion, I continued to correctly trace my state back to the right week, just the wrong part of the experience... To the floor of Sara's loft in Brooklyn instead of the pullout couch in Virginia.

I was given Valium and was checked back out. I saved the pills for the flight back to New York, the rest of that week is a blur. I can't even remember what happened on my mom's birthday. I know I met Jen and told her I needed more time to figure out what was going on. I know I called Maria and begged her to help.

I met Maria when I was about fifteen. She has no flashing florescent signs that hang in her living room window. She wears no turban, has no crystal ball. She is a middle-aged preschool teacher, a French Canadian from Montreal, a happy wife, battling the evils of M.S. My Aunt had heard of Maria through some friends. Maria does not advertise – she has no 900 number – no ad on Craigslist, but she is, undoubtedly an authentic medium. Maria is the only true psychic I know.

As soon as I heard her voice, I felt a sense of clarity that I hadn't felt for months. I did not speak, I only listened.

The first thing out of her mouth was a rhetorical question, she was laughing. She asked how in the world I thought I was going to live on this earth as just a head. She scolded me for ignoring my body for too long, that it was now coming back to bite me in the ass. She told me that she couldn't tell what exactly was attacking me at this point but assured me that it was only going to get worse.

She told me this was just the beginning of my entire world falling apart, but if I could hold on long enough, if I could survive, if I could get through to the other side, I had a chance to become a whole new person, not two disconnected parts.

She told me that this needed to happen at that moment. She said I had pushed myself to the limit and if I didn't break then, I'd break later.

I called Columbia University and set up an appointment with the school psychiatrist for the day after I got back...

They'd take care of me.

9 senioritis

After a Valium soaked plane flight – I ended up in the University building, Learner, that I had been in a hundred times. All of a sudden I was aware of the massive sheets of glass walls.

'*It was going to break wasn't it?*' I thought. '*Or I was going to fall through. Or jump. The giant windows… They're going to swallow me whole.*' I couldn't take the stairs, they were going to crumble beneath me. I couldn't take the elevator, it could constrict around me while I'm inside or decide to change directions and shoot me straight into the moon.

Everything everywhere had changed.

I no longer sat in the front row of the class. I sat in the back by the door in case I needed to run. I no longer took the subway, I knew the sickness could creep up on me from under the plastic bench seats, that the tunnels could collapse or fill up with water from the Hudson River and I'd drown. I could no longer walk the streets, I knew it could slide up from the cracks and wrap its way around my feet. It could sneak up on me anywhere and pull me under. It was hiding in my skin.

Terrified. Paralyzed.

My thoughts now interrupted my thoughts. I – *where* -

could – *am* – no – *I?*- longer – *What* - speak - *is* – without - *happening* – thoughts – *to* – interrupting - *me?* thoughts. All the persistent interruptions would force me to stop speaking mid

Where did all the words go? They used to be right there at the tip of my… of my… what the fuck is the name of that thing in my mouth? Words went missing leaving spaces on the shelves in my head, books checked out while the librarian overdosed and passed out on the tacky beige carpet behind the desk.

My only peace was blacking out, there was no longer such thing as sleep. Consciousness unbearable. Breaks between these episodes started slipping away more and more often, quietly, between the second and third hand of the clock when I wasn't looking. By October I found myself on the hard and cold wood floor of my apartment unable to move. There was nowhere left that was safe.

Tongue!

I opened my eyes and found myself in the psychiatrist's office with no memory of getting there.

"I think I've made a decision," I said calmly, my face near expressionless.
"Great, what's that?" He answered.

"I think I'm going to kill myself."

My mom was called and my roommates were asked to

watch me for the night as she flew into JFK on the redeye. My mom arrived to see a girl overcome by a sickness that was on a mission to conquer and destroy. That small part of me that told someone what I was planning to do was all I had left, that small part of me was fighting to stay alive *any* way it could.

I made extreme decisions for my own safety. My mom watched in disbelief as I, in a panic, insisted on gathering up every single knife and sharp object I had in my apartment and threw them down the garbage chute.

Only years later, after reading the news stories of suicides and murders committed by sufferers of advanced Lyme Disease, did I realize it may have been the smartest thing I ever did. Lyme shepherded me into a part of my brain I never in my life would have believed existed.

It felt like those knives had been calling me and I just couldn't look at them anymore. I would think about them while I lay in bed all night trying to sleep. I did not want to hurt anyone but all of a sudden I got the feeling that I should not put it past me. I didn't even really want to hurt myself. I held onto my wrists while I slept, I wrapped them with string and shoelaces, afraid they would act on their own accord. I placed them under the pressure of my body for protection. I was afraid I would cut my wrists open to get rid of the monsters that now lived inside me. I had a foreign entity eating me alive - chewing through my nervous system - piece by piece - destroying me from the inside out.

I'm not sure if I wanted to die - I just know I wanted to slice into my skin - enough to let the tainted blood run out. I imagined I could feel out the little bugs with my tongue and spit them out through my teeth like a mouthful of sesame seeds. There were bugs under my skin… what sane person wouldn't instinctively want to

GET THEM OUT.

• • • • •

My mom took a sabbatical from work and lived with me for over a month. She helped me get up every day. Made sure I ate. Tried to get me to classes. Sometimes she even sat in the back of the auditoriums with me for the large lecture courses. Only a year before, I had been hammering out 25 page papers for multiple masters/PHD courses, where I was the only undergrad allowed in. I was meeting with extraordinary men like Rubin "Hurricane" Carter and the head of the innocence project, Barry Scheck. I was having fascinating conversations with iconic historians like Eric Foner.

Now I could hardly remember how to take a shower.

There were short bouts where I would feel okay, a few hours where I felt normal again, but they didn't last long.

My mom and I shared my small room. I slept on the little couch that used to be Jen's. No matter how much I loved my two favorite shows, my mom could only take so much. She dragged me to the now extinct Blockbuster Video where I hesitantly picked out the documentary *Shut Up and Sing* about The Dixie Chicks to rent. Halfway through watching it I realized Blockbuster would have to literally come to my apartment and fist fight me if they ever wanted to get it back. I had *never* listened to "country" and yet now I insisted on pestering every nurse, doctor, neighbor, and Chinese food delivery-man to death about the brilliance of the film and my new admiration for this bad-ass named Natalie Maines.

My mom went with me to my school psychiatrist and psychologist. For months I had told them how bad things were getting. I told my psychiatrist, who was a dead ringer for Luigi from Mario Brothers, about the episodes of disorientation, the gnawing need to get out of my skin, the overwhelming fears, the lack of sleep, the piles of knives that I threw away from my kitchen.

When I had first come to see him he told me I had two choices:

I could pay a large amount of money as a co-pay to see him once in a while, and see another psychologist at almost full cost once every week or two.

Or, I could say that I had a problem with drug use and have my school insurance cover once a week sessions with him and two to three sessions a week with a psychologist for hardly any cost.

I had been prescribed Vicodin now and then over the

past year, but nothing serious. I hadn't actually taken any painkillers for months and I had not touched Adderall since the fourth of July. I caught his wink and decided to exaggerate greatly about these prescription drugs, reaping the benefits of low cost therapy. I figured if I was going to really dig into whatever hell was going on in my head, I needed as much help as I could get. I didn't have the money to do that without it being covered so I went along with it.

I didn't realize lying would highly damage the possibility of later bringing a malpractice suit to Columbia for misdiagnosing me and missing the Lyme disease. If anyone dug into my past for the case, they would see, admitted drug addict. The ridiculousness of the situation, even telling you now, never becomes less absurd.

My mom and I sat down with Dr. Luigi who prescribed me a heavy-duty tranquilizer, Clonazepam, a drug ironically enough commonly abused by true addicts. I was told to take it three times a day. This benzodiazepam has an extremely long half-life and was in my system at all times. He also prescribed me a high dose of Prozac, an antidepressant. He told me these episodes I was experiencing, the delusions, the itching to get out of my skin, was normal anxiety and depression caused by the stresses of senior year. It was commonplace to be worried about graduating, stepping into the responsibilities of the real world, it was simply... senioritis.

Brilliant.

I had never touched antidepressants or anti-anxiety medications in my life; I had actually been quite hard on people who did. I was under the impression that fear, depression, moods of all shades, were states of mind one could change through acceptance and reflection. It was a limited world view and an insulting one at that. It ignored the crisscrossing of circuits that nobody can think their way out of, not even good old pompous me. Still, to go along with this line of treatment was to go against *everything* I had believed in, and an admittance of how truly critical the situation was.

Of all the places to lose your mind, New York City may be the worst. You are constantly in the presence of people talking to themselves as you walk down the street. Every sick homeless person suddenly became me – my future – lying on a spit stained sidewalk, covered in filth, arguing with my own head.

I wrote letters to g-d and lit them on fire outside my window, my words begging for solace as they made their way in smoke up to the sky. If the answer was: I need medication because my brain can't handle my life changing again? So be it. Anything that came with a solution was fine with me.

The medications the psychiatrist prescribed slightly muffled the symptoms, enough to keep me constantly sedated. I tried going to class but couldn't get there often.

My honors average now became blemished with C's. My memory was fading fast. My professors and bosses were trying to be understanding but there was only so much they could bend.

The psychologist I met with three times a week sat twenty-five feet away from me across a dimly lit room in a chair facing mine. She never said a word till I spoke, a setup that could make anyone feel crazy, but in my state, was torture. I'd tell you what she looked like but she always sat too far away.

She asked me what it was I wanted to do in life. I told her I always had a plan, that since I was a kid I felt like I had a mission, that music was my way of having an impact on the world.

"A mission?" She would repeat back to me. "Like a mission from g-d?"

"I don't know," I'd answer, "like a purpose, maybe from g-d or the universe, or maybe just from watching *The Neverending Story* way too many times as a child."

"Does g-d tell you things?" She would continue.

"No, that's not what I meant. I meant I believe I have a place on this earth… that I have always had a place." I'd insist.

"Does g-d tell you to do bad things too? Does he ask you to hurt people?"

"What the hell are you talking about lady?" I'd respond as I watched her silhouette write down notes on her thick leather bound pad. Did she think I heard voices? Has she never met someone who believes they have purpose before?

"You have no idea who you are," she'd tell me. "You

have no idea."

"I know exactly who I am," I'd tell her. I *did* know. If I was ever anything I was the kid who was sure of herself. I was the girl who became a vegetarian at four years old and never wavered since. I was the kid who was so steadfast in her beliefs that she was sent to Washington D.C. on behalf of the Anti Defamation League at 15 years old, convinced her principal to shut down her high school for a day to let the Student Alliance For Equality take over all the classes at 16, and was asked to instruct the entire faculty in the district about discrimination at 17. I was the kid who always had a plan, who pursued music and politics with tenacity and focus, who believed in *loyalty* and *recompense*, and *justice*. I knew who I was.

But I was vulnerable and I was terrified. And I was also a girl who didn't know what was happening. I started wondering if maybe I had lost my mind. I even wondered if maybe I had actually died that night at Sara's and everything since then was a grand hallucination, some strange pre-heaven purgatory I was trapped in. Maybe I was frozen in a lucid dream gone terribly, terribly wrong.

Boy, that lady was a bitch.

As soon as I was properly diagnosed I called her up and gave her hell.

Many of the physical symptoms from Lyme were continuations from the symptoms I already have. I had already become used to the tendinitis so I didn't bother mentioning it to anyone. My insomnia was chalked up to anxiety as was the severe tremors I had developed in my hands. The physical fatigue and exhaustion were rationalized as symptoms of depression. I went to my school's GP with complaints of headaches, irregular heart palpitations and chest pains but these symptoms were brushed off as psychosomatic.

With my good luck, all the doctors at the University were tied together so I was already viewed as a mentally ill substance abuser before I even walked in the room. My fevers and sore throats were the only physical symptoms they took seriously. My mom went with me to my appointments, and reminded me about the tick bite in Virginia.

I told my GP. I was bit by a tick. She told me it couldn't be Lyme… She never even bothered to run the test.

Give me an F –A – N - T – A – S –T –I –C!
What does that spell? FANTASTIC!!!

My memory of that year, my head, looks like an old VHS some kid grabbed from his parents' cabinet. He played with the slow motion button and recorded over chunks of time with black and white blizzards circling through empty space. I know Mekia and Peter received couple housing and moved out. My mom stayed with me through the winter, till I was as stabilized as they thought I would be. I blinked and fall became winter, out of winter came hints of spring.

The only constant I remember was emailing back and forth with Kayden, the beautiful girl from the night in the Poconos. She had become my favorite distraction. For months we wrote each other almost every day.

The first email I wrote her was a risk for me, it was a moment of throwing caution to the wind, of pulling the car over in the middle of the highway to climb under barbed wire, lay in the grass, and take a picture. Irretrievable. I asked her some *very* important questions:

> *Would you rather sleep in a room that's very hot or very cold?*
> *Would you rather go to a club or go bowling?*
> *What do you think of astronaut ice cream?*

I asked her if she had a "boyfriend/girlfriend," I might as well have just sent her a note in crayon that said:

"Do you like boys or girls? Circle one."

I hit send and held my breath.

She answered me and I literally laughed out loud. She answered all my questions in-depth, with a surprising seriousness that was hilarious. Halfway through the email my mouth dropped open:

She was GAY!

What were the chances? Almost every girl I had ever had a relationship with was "straight" - well, formerly - which is honestly quite a compliment but sometimes a complicated pain in the ass. And now here was this girl who *knew* who she was! This girl was smart and creative, not only beautiful but had an obscure sense of humor. She was a girl I could fall in love with… and I would.

That year she was my lighthouse. She was far enough away to not see how I was out there, slowly becoming a crumbling version of what I once was... But she was still close enough to catch her light.

• • • • •

I flew back to San Diego from New York City, doped up on all three Clonazepam that Dr. Luigi told me to take throughout the six-hour flight.

I decided that when I arrived in San Diego I was getting my car and driving back. I needed my car in New York City. In the back of my mind I knew my life required an escape plan, and anyone plotting a get-away knows you need a pimp car waiting in the wings with its engine running.

Back at home in California, I saw my mom, got my car, and bought a dog.

Yeah, I don't really understand that part either.

I bought a great white Pyrenees, the largest, most amazingly inappropriate dog for an apartment in New York City you can find. I named him Junior. It ended up being one of the smartest things I ever did. My mom believed a dog would help me with my misdiagnosed depression and anxiety and help me get out of the house. She was still under the impression that I just needed to work a little harder, stop thinking so much, and try to focus my energy on something else.

Somehow, with only one day of notice, I convinced my friend and co-producer at the time Scott to drive back to New York City with me and Junior, who already weighed 50lbs at 11 weeks old. It was going to be my seventh time driving across the country.

The longest time I had spent getting from one side of the country to the other was three weeks. The shortest was approximately 42 hours, after my friend and I realized we weren't interested in seeing the same places along the way. I wanted to see the cities, he wanted to see the national parks; the only thing we could agree on was that we both wanted to see how fast we could make it across the country. With all his belongings in his grandmother's tiny '89 Toyota Camry –we sped across the land laughing and having oddly serious sleep-deprived arguments about my dislike of all things Lord of the Rings, and his love of triangles and the Pythagorean theorem.

No matter which trip it was, what car we took, or whom it was with… I had always been the primary driver. I was a machine. This time, I could hardly open my eyes.

I spent most of the trip in the back of the car sleeping with Junior. I woke up in Houston, tried to drive and hit another car. I woke up in New Orleans at four in the morning for beignets at Café du Monde. Covered in powdered sugar I walked Junior around the deserted Lafayette Square in my cowboy hat and bare feet hoping to find a tarot card reader

I had a run in with years before. I struck up conversations with a few homeless men, enjoyed the sticky humid air, got back in the car and went to sleep again.

I tried again to take over driving, but within minutes, for a fleeting moment, I fell asleep at the wheel. It was the first and only time that had happened to me. In those brief seconds of sleep I dreamt a semi was speeding towards me head on which startled me awake only to find that I had hit the brakes in my sleep and was almost at a full stop in the middle of a thankfully empty freeway. I pulled off at the next exit. Scott woke up in the passenger seat to find us parked behind an abandoned warehouse – Junior and I asleep in the back seat again.

I woke up in Georgia at Scott's friend's house. She and her family were born-again Christians. I treaded softly as I past an *entire* room dedicated to bibles and the complete "Left Behind" series – a chain of novels about the horrors non-believers will incur in hell if they do not accept Jesus Christ as their lord and savior. I kept my Jewish Canadian Queer mouth shut. I smiled with my teeth under a pair of cop-style mirrored glasses and the hood of a black torn sweatshirt I had been wearing since 7th grade when I took it from the lost and found.

The girl's mother emptied their refrigerator onto the counter – rolls, cookies, cheeses, meats, bags of chips, condiments, 3 types of mustard, nachos, milk, juice, fresh baked brownies and a cake lay out in front of us – in a much appreciated gesture of southern hospitality. It was a welcoming act that held a strange contradiction to the expression this woman wore on her face: fearful, condemnatory.

As we ate I was asked to leave Junior outside, so I rolled a few windows down part way and put him in the car with some water. When I got out a half hour later, he was gone. I was frantic. The house sat at the bottom of a dead end street that opened up into acre upon acre of pristine Georgia forest. As I started calling his name and got ready to head into the sea of trees, I looked down and there he was… sitting patiently next to the driver's side door. He had squeezed through the opening in the window and at only twelve weeks old, simply sat down and waited for me. I knew then why I had chosen him. He was loyal, like me. I loved him and he loved me back.

When we got to New York City my new assigned roommate had moved in and was less than thrilled about the surprise I brought home. The new girl was nerdy and uncomfortable, which wouldn't have been bad if she hadn't been pretentious about being nerdy and uncomfortable. She had ratty dirty blond hair that ended right below her waist. Her name was Anastasia. Who the hell is named Anastasia? She belonged at a renaissance fair. When she saw Junior for the first time, she freaked out and kicked him. He cried. I almost killed her.

I put up child gates in between the living room and kitchen in the apartment, I stayed on my side with Junior, she stayed on hers. We never spoke more than a few words again. I had a feeling I wouldn't be there long.

Junior made me laugh all the time; he still does. At

the time, he looked like a baby polar bear with giant feet sticking out from a ball of fluffy white fur. He was afraid of the stairs so I had to carry him up and down the 4 flights to my apartment. When I did try to walk him down he would stop and pee on people's doormats before I even had the chance to turn my head. He still has a knack for going to the bathroom in the wrong places like on parked cars. Recently he peed on someone's baby stroller when I wasn't looking.

We have a very similar sense of humor.

Junior is now two and a half years old, 185lbs, and comes up to my waist. If he stands up on his hind legs he is at least 6 ft. tall. He may just be the best friend I've ever had. If we ever run into Anatstasia again, he could eat her.

Through the spring semester, I found myself in the emergency room continuously. They put me on antibiotics, put me on a ventilator through the night to help with my shallow breathing, gave me an asthma inhaler and codeine syrup for my painful coughs.

Every time I was hospitalized or went to see the doctor I had a low-grade fever. These fevers would become my g-d-send, my only proof that my debilitated state was not the result of a sick mind's creation, it was real.

In April, my mom came out to check on me and Junior. We took my car up to Montreal to see family. On the way up I was in so much pain that we stopped at an emergency clinic in Lake George. They checked my throat and put me on antibiotics again. I was told I had another throat infection.

I told the doctor in Lake George I had been bit by a tick that past summer. He told me it couldn't be Lyme. He never even bothered to run the test.

While in Montreal I started throwing up and running an even higher fever. I missed the Passover Seder and dinner with the family, spending the night instead at the emergency room at St. Mary's Hospital. I was told this time I had gastro enteritis.

I told the doctor at St. Mary's I had been bit by a tick that past summer. She told me it couldn't be Lyme. She never even bothered to run the test.

We hit a snowstorm on the way back to New York City from Montreal and were forced to stay for three nights at a Best Western in Albany off the I-87. For the three days in the hotel I was completely unable to move from the bed. For the first time, my mom truly opened her eyes and watched. She saw how hard I was trying to read, trying to move, trying to do anything at all but couldn't. I was stuck. This wasn't depression. It wasn't anxiety. It was not a nervous breakdown. My body and my brain were fighting with everything it had against *something*:

And losing.

By the time we got back to New York City we both knew it was time to stop pretending I was stronger than this… that if I just tried a little harder I could rise above it, I could finish my classes like my peers, and I could graduate that fall like my friends.

It was time to pack up, drop out, and go home.

• • • • •

My mom flew back to San Diego. I sold my belongings and signed off on a semester full of incompletes. The night before I left, there was a knock on my door. I opened it to find Thaddeus, my former roommate holding himself up by the frame.

Thaddeus looked the way his name sounds. He was over 6 foot 3 with shoulder length curly dirty blonde hair, strong arms, and a chiseled face with its constant five o'clock shadow. Thad carried himself like a statue.

I met Thaddeus on the first day of orientation at Columbia. He sat next to me and my roommate Mekia. We ended up illegally renting our small spare room off the kitchen to Thaddeus under the table my first year there before Eric moved in. Thad and I stayed friends after he moved out, spending many nights listening to old school hip hop and playing on my original 1980's Nintendo. No matter what serious issue I brought up to Thad, he'd almost always find a way to incorporate references to 70's porn and professional wrestling into his answer or advice. It was a skill I had to respect. If I was having a hard time he'd distract me by insisting on playing me internet videos of strange men who were convinced they'd been abducted by aliens and rants about the Illuminati.

When I opened the door, I recognized the look on his face. He was having trouble breathing. He came in, lay down on the floor and closed his eyes. His heart was hurting, pumping up enough momentum to leave without saying goodbye. I asked him what happened, what he was on. He described the same mixture I had taken almost a year before, weed and a high dose of Adderall.

He asked me to call for help. I didn't reach for the fan.

I spent my last night in New York City watching as two paramedics carried the 220 lbs strong young man on a stretcher down four flights of steep cramped city stairs. We had taken the same amount of drugs and his blood pressure was 220/130. I could only imagine what *my* heart had gone through that July 4th night almost a year before. I sat in the back of the ambulance holding his hand. I stayed in the E.R. while they gave him a thick coal-like mixture to drink, ran tests, put in an IV, treated him well.

Four hours later, home from the hospital, Junior, Thaddeus, and I slept on the floor of my room where my mattress had been.

When we woke up Thaddeus told me those four sacred words:

You saved my life.

I didn't know what it would feel like to say those words to someone else.

But not to worry… Soon enough, I would.

10 lions v. bobcats

My mom and I began scouring San Diego proper for a diagnosis. I had found some kids on Craigslist who wanted to drive with Junior and me across the country in my car. My rashes returned. I became convinced with a new bright idea, 'I must have bed bugs!' I thought. So somewhere in the middle of New Mexico, traveling at eighty-five miles per hour on the Forty-West, I threw all of my pillows and blankets out the window.

We dropped one kid off in Tennessee; the other drove my car all the way to San Diego while Junior and I slept in the back. At one point Junior ate a butterfly. It was the most horrifyingly amusing thing I'd ever seen, his giant puppy face was oblivious as brightly multicolored flakes hung from the sides of his mouth. I still don't know either of the kids' names I drove with. All I know was that they had gas money.

At the first doctor I went to see, I passed out in the waiting room. The doctor was convinced my weakness was caused by mononucleosis and sent out my blood to be tested.

I passed out a lot. I passed out once at a party at my cousin's house after I told her I thought her husband looked like a goldfish.

I came to in time to hear a couple scolding my mom for not forcing me to eat meat – they blamed my symptoms on me being a vegetarian.

When my tests came back negative for mono, I was given antibiotics for strep again. I was then referred to a rheumatologist who diagnosed me with fibromyalgia "for the meantime" not actually believing that's what I had. He explained it fit some of my symptoms but didn't account for the fevers. He prescribed me meds to manage the joint pain and muscle aches while I continued to search for a diagnosis. When I got to his office I had asked him to turn down the lights in the examination room because my eyes had become very sensitive and I felt a headache coming on. By the end of the appointment, my head hurt so badly I couldn't even see straight. He looked over my records and between the blinding headache and my other symptoms he saw, he called the paramedics. He believed I had meningitis.

The lights and sirens howled as I was taken on a gurney from the doctor's office, into the ambulance, and straight to the emergency room at Scripps Hospital in Encinitas about twenty minutes away. The paramedics tried to comfort me but all I could say was "ouch."

My mom followed behind into the emergency room as they wheeled me in. The paramedics transferred me to a bed on the count of three and the doctors asked me to quantify my pain on a scale of one to ten. Spend enough time in a hospital and I swear you will start to ask just about everything in the parameters of one to ten.

"Let's get an LP setup please!" I heard the doctor order.

"What's an LP?" I whispered to the paramedic.

"They're going to perform a spinal tap honey, don't worry, you're going to be okay."

I watched him pack up and leave as a nurse helped me off the bed. They pulled down my jeans in the back and had me bend over the bed.

"Freezing the area now" the doctor said.

A needle of Lidocaine was stuck into my lower back. The nurse held my hand and I caught a glimpse of an even longer needle.

"Were going to extract a small amount of spinal fluid to test," she explained.

I took a deep breath as my lower back was wiped again with alcohol and then suddenly a large needle was stuck into the bottom of my spine. I tried not to vomit. The doctor shook his head at the empty needle, he had missed.

"One more time, deep breath please."

They missed again.

"Fuck!" I yelled out as my eyes welled up.

My head was still killing, my lower back felt like it wanted to run away. I started shaking uncontrollably without realizing it.

"You need to hold still okay?" The nurse told me.

"I'm trying," I whispered.

I couldn't stop shaking, the doctor handed the nurse a vile of Diazepam and she stuck a needle into my left arm to tranquilize me. My body relaxed and the doctor tried one more time. Tears rolled down my cheeks.

They extracted the fluid from my spine. I was forced to lay on my side while I waited for the results. I was clean for meningitis. I was hooked up to an IV and given morphine to relieve the pounding pain in my head and back. I fell asleep for a moment, finding temporary peace.

The new doctor in the emergency came on and was apparently not a big fan of mine. While reading my chart he asked where I went to school. He told me *he* went to N.Y.U. and that Columbia was his rival school. He was very serious. Luckily my mom and my brother were in the room to witness this outburst of his, otherwise I would have guessed I imagined it. His bitterness grew after that, assuring there was nothing wrong with me. He then proceeded to tell me that even if I had cancer, he would not admit me to the hospital. I told him I wasn't moving. My mom went ballistic on him.

It was two a.m. but I waited there on the gurney 'till the next doctor came on at six a.m. Luckily my brother, who met us there, found a little DVD player in my mom's car and we watched *Little Miss Sunshine* until the new doctor arrived. Within five minutes of examining me and taking my history he checked me straight into the infectious disease ward.

I was wheeled into a private room where I was put through a slew of tests, Cat scans, MRIs, EKGs. I was poked and prodded more times than I could count. I had to pee in clear cups and shit into red plastic containers.

I was in a hospital room that overlooked the highway. I

could see the same underpass that I used to climb up in high school during lunch. I'd climb to the top of the cement wall and sit in the middle of the highway to drink my 7-11 coffee among the brush between the north and southbound lanes; in the middle of freeway, watching thousands of people fly by at seventy, eighty plus miles per hour on either side, I was completely invisible.

My hospital room was about five blocks away from Jen. I called her to tell her I was there in the hospital. She never came to visit.

I was surprised.

We had been close friends for almost twelve years. That was the last time we ever spoke.

I have seen her now and again though... in between reruns of *Roseanne,* Jen flashes on the screen in fifteen to thirty second frames - talking about her armpits and hawking Dove deodorant. I awake at times to her voice in the middle of the night when I've left my TV on too loud after passing out from my third IV infusion. She flashes on the screen for those seconds as nothing more than the face of a ghost, a haunting from another life, a life that I can hardly remember what it felt like to live.

Doctors piled into my hospital room. Interns surrounded them, watching me with their pens held steady. I felt doubted, humiliated, and spoken down to. My mom and brother came by but they had to work. Mostly I was alone. Every night I watched my reruns on my mini DVD player.

Some nights I 'd sneak down to the cafeteria where I'd get the janitor to break the rules and buy me some ice cream.

I insisted on being taken off the Prozac and Clonazepam. I had been on nine rounds of antibiotics since January, which was the real reason my depression and states of panic had heavily subsided. It was now June and after two weeks of being in the infectious disease ward, the hospital was still pulling at straws. I was sick, that was clear to all of us. My once white arms were bruised from needle marks, from pulling blood to test. My forearms were full of small black and blue circles that formed the bottom half of hundreds of question marks.

"So... what is it?"

I had a documented fever for almost a year now – the pain had spread everywhere, the exhaustion had become relentless.

"All we got was another positive culture on your throat for staph... and the ultrasound shows your spleen is enlarged," The doctor explained. "Now, your spleen could be inflamed from the infection in your throat or there could be an infection in your spleen. We can't biopsy the spleen without taking it out which we are strongly considering. But I would like to start with taking out your tonsils first."

I always thought getting your tonsils taken out would be like you see on TV: Lots of ice cream, popsicles, movies, and sleep...

Bull freaking shit.

I didn't even make it three blocks home before I puked blood all over the side of the road.

I spent all of June recovering from surgery in the most excruciating pain I had ever known, finding comfort only in my rare morphine induced black outs. I'd wake up screaming, hacking up chunks of blood. Maybe the recovery from a tonsillectomy is that bad. Or maybe the fact that it was a completely unnecessary surgery or that my body was a little busy fighting off a completely *different* illness made it so much worse... but Jesus Mary and Josephine Carter, it was fucking awful.

The fourth week after surgery rolled around and my antibiotics were finished. My mom drove me to my last visit at the Ear Nose and Throat doctor. He checked my throat. It had healed perfectly. He checked my temperature.

It was a hundred and one.

11 july 4th, 2007

A year and an entire coast away from Brooklyn, I stood looking out my old bedroom window at my mom and her friends; a crowd of sweet middle-aged cowgirls sitting around a patio table eating barbeque and drinking Diet Coke and Canada Dry. The American flag waved indifferently above the dry canyon behind our house. The ocean sat silent a few miles away. I always enjoyed living on the edge of the continent – I could always find myself easily on a map.

My phone rang.

"Hello?" I answered, still worn.
"Hi." I heard a timid voice, "It's Kayden."
I was stunned. After dropping out of school, moving home, being hospitalized, and recovering from surgery, here she was again.
I sipped some leftover morphine from a shot glass.
"Umm…" I was immediately tongue-tied again. "Hi! Where have you…? We've never, um… we've never spoken on the phone before."
"I know," she said. "I thought it was about time."

I was wrapped up in her voice immediately. I fell back

on my bed and listened. We talked for hours, till the sun went down outside my window and the fireworks exploded over the canyon behind my house.

I awaited appointments with more specialists and was too sick to do nearly anything else so every moment I could spend talking to Kayden I did.

My insomnia coincided with her getting up early so we talked every morning on her way to work, seven a.m. her time, four a.m. mine. We texted each other all day and laid in bed talking all night. Days fell off the calendar like delicate flowers, softly landing on my bed in bright colors till my fingers could run over them – till I could grab them in fistfuls and blow them into the air.

She told me all her secrets. I had all the time in the world to listen. Most days I couldn't leave my room, but I no longer hated it, as long as I was talking to her. I gave her an open heart to confide in and one day she began to share with me the weight she had been carrying around her neck, the abuses she had suffered as a child. Stories she had never shared with anyone.

I had no idea how much damage had been done till one day in late August she called crying so hard she could hardly speak. Something had set her off and she broke. Her words indiscernible from tears, she told me she couldn't take it anymore. I was in shock. She was driving. I could hear the speeding highway behind her voice. I knew she was thinking of driving herself right off the road. I said everything I could to calm her down, to let her know she wasn't alone. I finally convinced her to pull over the car.

I then told her the one thing I had begged her not to say since the day we had met because I knew I wouldn't believe her…

I told her I loved her.

I could feel her pain break for a moment over the phone. She said those three words back to me.

"I love you," she said clearly smiling, her tears finally fading. When I was convinced she was okay, I let her go.

She called me back minutes later to tell how long she had wanted to say those three words to me and repeated them over and over as if the door she'd been banging on had been locked and was now finally open. She then told me those *four* words I'd really rather not hear so much:

"You saved my life," she said.

She booked a flight to California, she was coming out to see me.

My cheeks were numb. There weren't enough red flags in the world smacking me across my face that could have stopped me from getting into a relationship with that girl. I could practically hear the reverberating *ping* from the metal flag poll hitting me over the head. Perhaps I was colorblind. Perhaps I didn't know the flags were red, maybe I thought they were white, some kind of sign to let go of all the walls I'd built up all those years, some kind of sign to surrender.

Plus, there was definitely something about saving someone else that created the perfect diversion from the battle I was losing for my own life. I should have never doubted we'd end up together...

The sick beget sick, always.

The Kayden who came to California was just like the girl from the first emails, caring and funny, beautiful and intense... no sign of the incident in the car weeks before. I rested for days to save up enough energy to pick her up from the airport. I arrived as speechless as the day we met.

"I got lost... sorry. I can't drive much." I practically whispered when I arrived late to an airport I'd been to hundreds of times.

"I forgot how quiet you are in person," she smiled and took my hand as we drove.

"The beach?" I asked in a mumble.

"The what baby?" She hadn't understood me.

"You want to go to the beach?"

"Now? Yeah, sure!"

I was near silent as we drove towards the ocean. We got out at Moonlight Beach and sat in the dark by the shore together. I dragged my fingers through the soft sand, drawing circles, staring at the same waves I had been watching since I was a child. I only got out a couple words at a time.

"What are you thinking?" She asked.

"Sit here." I said softly and patted the patch of sand in front of me.

"What?"

Shit. She hadn't heard me again.

"You," I said a little louder, "sit here."

She smiled and got up, then sat back down in front of me. I wrapped my arms around her waist. She leaned back into me and my eyes filled up with tears.

"Jesus Christ… I am so tired," I whispered.

Life had become so unrecognizable, so frightening, as doctor after doctor left me empty-handed and sent me on my way. I wanted answers but at that moment everything stopped. I could let go.

In a world where you are constantly floating, where gravity is no longer doing its job, there is nothing like the weight of another body to keep you grounded. All I needed was this girl to hold, the weight of her body against me. This stranger I loved that would love me back. Touching her let all my fear and sorrow leave me for just a moment.

She turned herself around – putting her delicate hands around the back of my neck, she kept her soft blue eyes on mine as her fingers slid up slowly through my hair. She kissed me for the first time. Neither of us had any plan to stop again.

I had been sexually involved with people but at the time I met Kayden, I was a virgin. I was the last of the Donna Martins. It had nothing to do with religion, just a belief that sex was something sacred, not something I was ready to share with just anyone. Kayden knew all of this and I knew I'd have to make some choices when she got there. The morning before she flew in, I called Thaddeus back in New York for his advice.

"I want you to just consider something seriously for a second okay?" He said in a deep and thoughtful voice.

"Okay, shoot." I awaited his one of a kind wisdom.

"Well, you're pretty much still dying right?"

"Yes Thad, thank you, I forgot how sensitive you are!"

"So," he continued, "Just consider for a second that the Muslim extremists have been right all along. Now, according to them, if a Muslim dies in the name of Allah like a suicide bomber let's say, then he receives seventy-two virgins when he gets to heaven. If you die from whatever disease is killing you, you'll die a virgin, and that means *if they're right* you'll have to spend *eternity* fucking an old middle-eastern man with a giant beard. Are you *really* willing to take that risk?"

Kayden and I left the beach and slept together for the first time that night.

Sex with Kayden was everything I believed it could be. Intense. Alive. The hypnotic sounds of Sigur Ros filled the air in my room from the speakers surrounding my bed. Sex with Kayden was as loving and reverent as it was powerful. It was sex of desperation. It was sex in search of a savior. I could have lived off nothing but.

Kayden pulled the covers over both our heads as the moonlight snuck through the corners of the blinds and lit up the bright whitewashed cave of sheets we hid under. I could feel her breath against the side of my face.

"Since I never officially asked," she whispered, I felt her mouth form a smile and hit my cheek. *"Will you be my girlfriend?"*

I found her lips and kissed them.

"I thought I already was."

We didn't leave my room for nearly three days. We had each lost about five pounds by the time she had to go home… I was never much of a fan of moderation.

I believed I could not have waited for anything more. We were in love and it was all I needed.

12 are you counting my calories?

The doctors I saw all believed I had something different, the only thing they had in common was that 99% of the diseases they tested me for had no cure.

My white blood count was off so they thought I had cancer. Some thought lupus. I was put through bone marrow aspiration by the oncologist I was sent to. I walked slowly, exhausted, passing the cancer patients sitting in their individual lazy boys being pumped with Chemo, just like my mom had once been. Hair gone, eyes sunken back and spent… just like my mom had once looked. I was terrified that I was next.

The thick bone marrow needle was shoved deep into my right hip during the procedure. I tried not to scream. I swear, if you haven't already seen how long these needles are, I hope you never do.

The only thing distracting me was Kayden. There is nothing as powerful to detract from the pain of these procedures than getting naked photos of your girlfriend text to you. Nothing better to pass away the lonely hours of insomnia-filled nights than phone sex. Love and human touch, sex of any kind can relieve pain in a way no opiate or tranquilizer can touch… believe me, I've been prescribed them all.

I tested negative for cancer.
I tested negative for M.S.
I tested negative for H.I.V.

I was getting worse but I had stopped caring. Still limping from the bone marrow needle, I began packing my suitcase. After a long talk with my mom, she understood that I needed to go to Pennsylvania.

"I don't know what the right thing to do is," I told her. "But... I feel like I've missed so much already. The truth is we don't know what's going to happen or how long I'm going to be... you know... I just don't want to miss anymore."

My mom understood the urgency. She was comforted that my brother who had just moved out to New York City for a job would not be far away if I needed anything.

I decided if I was going to be stuck in bed 95% of the day, it might as well be Kayden's. I had enough painkillers for six weeks and enough tranquilizers to get me there and back so I doped myself up and got on another plane, this time to Pennsylvania.

When Kayden met me at the airport, I didn't recognize her. She probably believed it was the illness messing with my memory but it wasn't. I didn't think much of it at the time but I knew deep down I didn't recognize her because part of me never really cared who she was. I was in love with someone holding my hand through the nightmare that had become my life... if I had really been paying attention I would have never let her get so close.

Kayden and I lived with her parents in her childhood home. The house was both peculiar and cold. Each night we ate dinner on TV trays in the living room in silence minus the few unenthusiastic laughs over the reruns of *Becker.* They watched episodes over and over making little comments now and then like, "Do you think that black fellow is really blind?"

Kayden was still forced to drink a glass of milk and have a slice of bread with each meal. Her mother was quiet and a little dowdy, she taught preschool for children with disabilities. Her father was a bishop at the local church. Kayden told me her father had hit her when she was younger. When the school came by with social services to investigate her bruises and black eye, she told me her mother, like many weak women of the world, protected her man instead of her child.

The house was in Easton, Pennsylvania, the same town where a couple named their child Adolph Hitler and then wondered why people around the world were displeased. Kayden's parents didn't know we were a couple, or pretended they didn't. When I got there I found out we were supposed to sleep in two small twin beds in her bedroom. We had to set an alarm at five a.m. every morning so I could switch out of her bed and into the other one before her parents walked in….

And they did walk in, every morning. They walked in all the time. There was no lock on our door. The mom once walked in as Kayden was pulling her hand out from the front of my jeans, who knows what lie she told herself to justify that one. Other than the silent dinners they really didn't seem to notice my presence. I believe once in six weeks they came upstairs during the day to ask how I was feeling. It was all quite disconcerting.

I was the only person outside the three of them that knew the secrets of the family, the abuse nobody had ever spoken about; making living there even more uncomfortable than it already was. I began to learn that was Kayden's M.O.; She never confronted her attackers - she lived with them. She lived as a 23 year old with her father who she still walked on eggshells around, always terrified to upset him. Before that she had lived with an ex-girlfriend who hit her.

While there I also found out she had lived with a male friend who one night raped her. It was a terrible trauma that is not at all my story to tell, however, I did find out that she suffered the rape one week before I met her that night at Perkins. I finally understood the full picture of that night, of the search her heart was on when she made eye contact with me as she walked through the door, I now understood her pull to take a risk, to sit down at the booth next to me.

I was the *only* person who knew any of this had happened. I was the *only* person who knew she had tried to kill herself. I knew a lot of things I shouldn't have; too many things for one person to know.

To drive the dysfunctional red flag into the ground, I found out while there that Kayden was also a recovering bulimic.

Yes, it all scared me… but to be honest, I knew I wasn't going anywhere.

Kayden had told me her eating disorder was under control but someone obsessed with food is never easy to live with. I tried to ignore it. Having spent most of my pre-sick days in the entertainment world, I had become accustomed to these types of people and resorted simply to joking that I wouldn't bother paying for dinner if she was just going to throw it up after.

Someone with an eating disorder doesn't focus solely on what goes into her mouth, but on what goes into the mouths of everyone else around them. I could see her watch as I poured my cereal or drank a cup of soy-milk. I finally asked her flat out once,

"Are you counting my calories?"

She didn't bother to lie or be ashamed about it.

"Of course," she said.

I didn't even see the flag anymore - it had grown so big that it covered my world like a tent. I walked around in a perpetual red-tinted sunset.

Kayden and I lived a secret life in that home, one neither of us had ever known. She went to school while I stayed in her room and slept all day. I could still walk a little so when I had the energy I would. We would lie in bed at night fantasizing about our future together. We made promises to each other. One night she said she had a surprise.

We drove through the thick forest of the Poconos. We were quite the pair when it came to being in the car together. Kayden was as intensely gripped by music as I. Every nuance caused an isolated reaction. The deep hit of the kick drum translated to the side of a fist smacked against the steering wheel, a flat palm with a snare, a nod of the head, a turn of the shoulders… every note mattered, every sound was felt.

We pulled up to the Perkins parking lot. We held hands as we walked through the door and took a seat at the third booth down on the right. Kayden took out a folder full of our e-mails, she had saved every one of them.

We ordered the worst grilled cheese in the world and read through the emails together laughing at all our pathetic attempts at flirting. Both of us had been trying so hard throughout that first year of writing to let each other know we were interested but we were both so terrible at showing it then. Kayden then took out a smaller piece of paper from her wallet… it was the original receipt from Perkins with my number and email on the back. She had kept it right there since that night far over a year before. She told me not a single day went by where she hadn't thought about me, even when she would disappear now and then, I was always on her mind.

I couldn't help but ask the question that had been haunting me since the first night we talked.

"What if this is all I am?" I asked.

"What do you mean?" She replied.

"What if this is it? What if I never get any better? I don't even know if I could get my career back if I tried, what if I never become a *famous* musician or an Ivy League graduate, what if this is all I ever will be…"

"That never mattered to me," she said taking my hands.

She told me that she didn't care if I ever graduated. She told me that as much as she loved my voice, she didn't care if I never played another song in my life. She made sure I was listening. She spoke slowly.

"I am not in love with some version of who you could have been," she assured me, keeping her eyes on mine, "I am in love with *you*. I know you have been alone but you aren't going to be alone anymore, I am not going *anywhere*."

Nobody had ever said such things to me. Nobody ever told me that even if I wasn't doing anything of great worth I would still be worthy… nobody ever made me feel like I could stop fighting so hard. Nobody ever made me feel like I was safe just being a girl instead of always a girl with the potential for being something so much greater.

For someone like me to be told I would never be alone again, was a moment more overwhelming, terrifying, and beautiful than anything I'd ever heard in my life. She wouldn't let my hands go until I actually allowed myself to believe her. And I did.

Late at night, as I was falling asleep against her, Kayden asked me what kind of ring I wanted someday.

"What kind of ring?" I repeated startled.

"*Oh shit. I said that out loud? …I'm so embarrassed.*" Kayden buried her face in the pillow, "*I'm sorry I'm sleeping, I'm sleeping.*"

"What ring? What are you talking about baby?"

Through the muffled sounds of the pillow her voice came through, "*When I propose?*"

There in the dark she told me all the ways she planned on proposing. She told me how she was going to set up a picnic some night at one of my favorite spots, the roof of the School of International and Public Affairs building across the street from my old apartment where you could sneak up and see the whole New York City skyline. She told me she was going to hide the ring in a package of astronaut ice cream.

With a serious shyness she asked, "Do you think you'll say yes?"

In that cool dark Pennsylvania air I couldn't stop smiling. "…Yes."

We spent many nights talking about the names for the kids we wanted to have someday. We picked out the song we wanted to walk down the aisle to, the one we wanted to have our first dance to.

After about six weeks out there, I had to go back to San Diego to see my doctors. I knew I was getting worse, the spaces in between the moments where I was too tired to even fully open my eyes, at times to even speak, were becoming shorter and shorter as the days passed. The painkillers I was on no longer put a dent in the extraordinary physical pain I was in. Kayden and I made plans that she would move in with me after she graduated from East Stroudsburg at the end of the fall semester, only a little more than a month away. It would be the first time she would live farther than twenty minutes away from her parents, from her friends, from the rural land in the outskirts of Easton, Pennsylvania. She would leave her job, her family, her home, and move three thousand miles away to be with me.

For some reason this sounded familiar – but my brain was too tired to climb up the ladder and ring that bell.

Every time I think about living out there with her, every memory I have is cut by the view of morning out her second story window; Her front yard, and across her street, an empty field of wet grass. I can remember how it felt to kiss her when she got home from work – her lips were always so cold at first from being out in the winter coming fast. I can remember the silence of the house and the way her hair smelled when she came out of the shower. I remember how her body felt on top of me in the dark after her parents finally went to sleep. Yet every memory is cut by the lawn, where in the mist of each late October morning stood a family of deer. Deer that stared back at me through the small upstairs window. Deer that by all likelihood carried a disease, the same disease that was killing me.

It was staring right at me and I never saw a thing.

13 soothsayers and superbowls

Lyme has immense cyclical flare ups. Usually every four weeks things get really bad but there are times throughout the month when sometimes you feel better, even random days when you think you're going to be okay. On those good days, it was easy to trick yourself into thinking everything was fine again! I would think the worst was over. I'd push myself and then later be worse for the wear. I'd want to go out. I'd want to go anywhere, even just the grocery store.

One night I walked carefully through the giant aisles of Costco – holding onto the piles of boxes for support. Most days now I couldn't walk without holding onto something.

I stepped carefully until I reached the surfboards. I decided I was going to get better suddenly, and I was going to surf. Everyday! I might even let my skin tan, and my hair go blonde from the salt water and sun! The next thing I remember was two employees helping me into a wheelchair and handing me a free bottle of Costco water to drink. I still *insisted* on buying that surfboard. One pushed me slowly to the register while the other held the long blue board under his arm. My mom found me up front at the register and took me home.

I'm still waiting to be strong enough to surf.

I had pushed myself flying to Pennsylvania, within a week of getting home from Kayden's house I was rushed into the hospital again.

They admitted me into the infectious disease ward of U.C.S.D.'s Thorton Hospital down in La Jolla, California. I was put through the same extensive run around. I was screened and tested. Blood was drawn over and over again. Sahba, a family friend was in the room when they sent in the new nurse who was trying to set up a new IV line. She couldn't find a good vein left on my arm so she tried my hand. She hit the vein wrong and blood sprayed everywhere, all over the bed, all over my arm, all over her, into the air. I laughed out loud while this poor little Asian nurse panicked in circles around me as she tried to backtrack her mistake. Sahba was laughing too. Luckily the one friend who came to visit had the same sick sense of humor I did.

Two long weeks passed in the hospital, the examinations were exhausting, the outlook was dim. I heard my mom whispering on the phone outside my door talking to my brother:

"Where the hell is everyone? Did you email Mary or Katherine, anyone to let them know how sick she is? …No I don't give a shit if they're scared of hospitals, Steve, she's all alone…"

The head of infectious disease interrupted her. My mom followed her into the room. The doctor told me they had hit a wall. She told me she was sure that I was sick, that the fevers were real, that my symptoms were clear, but that she did not know what it was. Her answer? She hoped that eventually whatever it was would manifest, but in the meantime I should just live this way and be discharged with "fever of unknown origin."

She left the hospital room. I sat on the bed, wondering what to do next.

I told my mom to pass me the hospital phone, I was going to call Maria.

I dialed.

"You have Lyme Disease."

There was no "hello." No "who is this?" The phone went straight from ringer to answer. I was just hoping she would pick up.

"Maria? Do you know who this is?" I asked her.

"Of course," she answered. "And you have Lyme Disease."

"It's impossible," I told her. "They have run a million tests. I'm sure they must have tested me for Lyme."

"They screwed up," she insisted. "Remember the summer before last? You left New York and went to another state remember? For work? For music? You got bit by a tick there! (I had never told her a thing.) You have Lyme disease. Now get the hell out of that hospital. They don't know what they're doing there."

I hung up the phone and called back the doctor in one last ditch effort before I was to be released. I told her

I believed my symptoms resembled Lyme and that since I had been bit by a tick I should be tested.

She told me she didn't believe that Lyme disease exists.

• • • • •

Kayden graduated from college and was packing for her move out at the start of the New Year. For Christmas I sent her a jewelry box with a copy of the key to my house inside. Christmas and my birthday passed, I didn't get anything back. I told myself she was busy.

I was excited to show her the new furniture I had for what was now *our* room. I had gotten help and had the wall painted her favorite color, Carolina Blue. I had cleaned out what were now *our* dressers. I had made room for her things. When she arrived I knew she was not okay, or maybe for the first time I really let myself see it.

I sat down on my bed and watched as Kayden went straight to unpacking.

"You doing alright?" I asked.

"Yep, just taking it all in."

"You sure?"

Kayden walked over and kissed me unconvincingly. She began unpacking again.

After a week she finally broke down and told me what was wrong. She had run into the guy who had raped her a few days before she flew out. She decided she wanted to tell me what had happened the night he raped her, details she had yet to disclose to anyone. As soon as she started to go into detail part of me knew I was trapped.

Everyone has their patterns in life, kinds of relationships or behaviors that follow them no matter how much work on themselves they seem to do, something perhaps cosmic, banging the same situation against one's skull over and over again until they have some sort of epiphany. Some would say I was like Brandon Walsh, always having a thing for wounded birds, as the great Emily Valentine once observed.

I think for me it went a step further. My life's pattern was meeting people who wanted to confide in me about things they have never told to a soul on earth. Since I was a kid people often felt drawn to tell me dark things about their lives, feelings they never let themselves admit before, dreams they had never said aloud but wished they could. These people always felt so close to me at first. However, if that person was not ready to deal with the truths they had revealed, that closeness they felt for me changed drastically – my knowing, even silently, became something they despised.

By the time Kayden and I met, I had already been told by *four* separate people that I had literally saved their life. I never wanted that kind of power. Sometimes those four words were the last I ever heard that person say to me again. I would become a mirror for someone who was not ready to see, a reminder of all the secrets they weren't ready to face. I was a steppingstone to acceptance, and it happened over and over again. And over and over again I let myself be used.

My epiphany?

Well, Kurt Vonnegut Jr. said it best in *The Sirens of Titan*. "The worst thing that could possibly happen to anybody, would be to not be used for anything by anybody."

That was the most meaning I could ever find.
Still, it blew.

I didn't fully realize this was what was slowly happening between Kayden and me at the time, but it was.

I spent a week calling everyone I could think of who might know a Lyme specialist. I started through my list of doctors I'd seen, they came back with no ideas, no referrals. Nobody could even point me in the right direction, finally I got to the last name on my list.

The receptionist answered. I went through my customary shpeal.

"How about that girl on the news?" She laughed.

"What girl?" I asked her. "Was there a story about someone with Lyme?"

"No, no," she continued amused that I was seriously interested, "There's this woman who does the weather on channel five or six or something? She talks every once in a while about having Lyme disease."

I paused for a moment.

"You think I should talk to the weather girl?" I asked her.

"Who knows, I don't have any other ideas."

"Well," I told her, "I'm going to go find the weather girl."

"Okay…" She laughed. "Good luck!"

I googled "weather girl with Lyme" and found local forecaster Brooke Landau. Within two days of calling her office, I received a kind and in depth explanatory email from her that included a list of the most renowned Lyme specialists throughout the country, the specific blood tests I needed to ask for, the treatment that worked for her, and the contact info for the doctor who saved her life. She offered her ongoing support, if needed, during my treatment and offered herself as a reference.

I made an appointment with the leading specialist on the west coast that had treated her. I'd go up to see him in February. In the meantime he set up an in depth blood test for Lyme through another doctor at Cedar Sinai Hospital in Los Angeles that week.

After a year and a half of sickness, with bated breath I awaited the results. My last resort.

The end of January rolled around. Kayden and I had spent the month living together at my mom's home. Kayden was anxious about finding a job, she ran twice a day for hours at a time.

"You training for an Iron Man I don't know about babe?" I'd ask as she unlaced her running shoes for the second time that day.

"Just keeping busy." She'd smile weakly,

"You trying to keep busy from me?" I finally asked.

"Of course not!" She assured me with a sparse kiss on the cheek, sitting back at her computer to look for jobs again.

One day she came in with a spark of excitement I hadn't seen in weeks.

"You'll never believe this!" She exclaimed, "My friend from Easton just called… she's living in Phoenix and just got a job for the Super Bowl!"

"Congratulations friend from Easton!" I yelled back as a joke.

"No, they found an extra job for me! I get to work at the Super Bowl!"

She loved football, which I thought was adorably gay of her.

"I'll only be gone a week," she continued.

"I think that sounds perfect for you."

I was excited for her. I thought it would do us good to take the week for ourselves. I let her borrow my car, my prized possession, my 1983 Oldsmobile - Delta 88 Royale. We kissed against the car in my driveway.

"I know you're going through a lot right now," I said, "But you should know something."

"What's that?" She asked.

"I'm totally fucking in love with you…" I told her smiling, "But seriously, don't fuck up my car."

She got into the driver's seat and we kissed goodbye through the open window.

"*I love you too,*" she whispered.

I watched her pull out of the driveway and up my street.

Her last day of work at the Super Bowl rolled around and a message alert went off on my phone. A cold, three-word, text from her appeared in the message box:

Check your email.

I did.

I opened her email and as I scanned through it I felt myself fall onto the floor. She said something along the lines of being afraid I knew too much, of being homesick, and of not being well enough herself to be there for me, of not being able to love me anymore.

By the time I received the email she was already in New Mexico. She had left my car in Arizona. Someone I didn't know would apparently, at some point, bring it two hours away to Los Angeles where I could find a way to come get it. Kayden had gotten in a different car with a friend from school and was already on her way back to her parent's house in Pennsylvania.

She had left her computer and her clothes. Her favorite hooded sweatshirt, books, and Panteene Pro V shampoo. She had left our Burberry scented pillows she had sprayed with her expensive perfume to make sure I didn't forget the way she smelled that week while she was away. She had left our matching dressers. She had left her fresh painted Carolina blue wall. She had left all the promises she ever made.

She had left me.

I laid on the floor till the following morning. My cell phone rang and woke me up.

My test results were in:
Positive for multiple Lyme related co-infections.
Positive for multiple strains of Lyme.

14

i became a superhero and all i got was this lousy t-shirt

I awaited my meeting with Dr. Harris, my specialist.

I was sent a huge chunk of forms my mom helped me fill out to prepare me for my appointment. It made me aware of all the odd symptoms I had developed over the past year and a half that I hadn't even realized were symptoms at all.

I hadn't even recognized that something extraordinary had happened. I had become a superhero. I had super senses.

And guess what?

Super senses sucked.

My ears were magic - Spy sensory devices. The volume knob in my head was turned up – then accidentally broke off.

I had instinctively created a white noise trifecta in my room; air conditioner, fan, and television. But I could still hear everything. Even the clicking... the tap; tap-tap-tapping. It would retreat than return. I turned off the TV. I turned off the air. I turned off the fan. I began my hunt. I followed the tap; tap-tap-tapping. I was on a mission to destroy.

There! I was getting closer!

TAP!!!!! TAP! TAP! TAP!

I found it!

The sound that was rising above all the piles of noise – white and otherwise – the sound distracting me, aggravating me, infuriating me, was the minuscule sounds of the cable box… working.

I cried at the sound of a soda can opening in front of me. That tssss CRACK! The sound of hundreds of baby carbon dioxide bubbles gasping for air as they escape felt like dynamite being let off in my eardrum.

My mom tried to distract me from my misery. She took me to a throwback diner to get a bite to eat.
"I have to leave. I'm sorry." I said minutes after the food arrived.

"But you haven't even taken two bites yet," my mom answered as she tried to find my eyes.

I sat slouched in the booth at the restaurant with my hands over my ears, my elbows propped against the table. My big white-rimmed sunglasses helped block out the light. I may not have had control of much, but at least I could still wear whatever on earth I wanted. I sat there bouncing my legs anxiously. I was wearing a pair of white long underwear, bona fide long johns with the front flap and all. They were covered in little tiny black electric guitars. I wore them tucked into a pair of glistening gold cowboy boots I found at a second hand store for only fourteen bucks. What a steal. I was wearing my same comfy v-neck faded dark grey t-shirt and a blue striped hooded sweatshirt – a second line of defense from the bright lights. I didn't even bother to put my arms through the sleeves; I wore it hung over my head and back, like a cape.

"I can't stand the noise," I told my mom without removing my hands from my ears. I stared at an uneaten perfectly decent diner style veggie burger and an untouched cherry chocolate shake. I had high expectations that night. I thought I might actually be hungry... but, the noise...

"What noise?" My mom asked, confused.

"Don't you hear it?" I was getting frustrated. "The shhhhhhhhhhhhhhh…. It won't stop."

There were children crying at the booth next to us. There was a toy train loudly circling on a track that hung from the ceiling. The restaurant was packed with people talking. I could hear accents from out-of-towners who came to eat down the street from the land made out of Legos; the sad excuse for entertainment in this town. Apparently it was necessary to build an amusement park near our house that features miniatures of places all over the world that are more amusing than here. I would have been happy if somebody had just finally opened up a damn bowling alley! Valerie Malone was right, these people are such a bunch of avocado heads.

SHHHHHHHHHHHHHHHHHHHHH

Nothing could drown it out.

My mom excused herself to the restroom that was located at the other side of the restaurant near the kitchen. I sat picking at my plate. When she returned she grabbed my hand and asked me to follow her back from where she came. She stopped me at the kitchen.

"Is that the noise?" She asked.

It was.

Over thirty feet away from the booth we had been sitting at. Coming from the back of the kitchen, from behind the doors, was the noise that had rose up in my head enough to drown out all others and ruin my meal:

It was the sound of the fries, cooking.

It wasn't just my hearing, all of my senses were new. The tiny sensory hairs on the inside of my nose were electrocuted – they stood up straight searching for the smallest scent to sound the alarms.

One night I was awoken by the pungent smell of peanut butter. I couldn't figure out where it was coming from. The air conditioning was on, as was the fan. My Yankee Café au Lait candle was still burning; but had disappeared in the shadows of the overpowering peanut butter jar from hell.

I checked the vents, they were closed! The only opening to the rest of the house is the small crack under the door to my room. I was a child who has been woken from her first restful sleep in weeks.

"WHY DOES EVERYTHING SMELL LIKE PEANUT BUTTER?!"

I screamed at the ceiling, at the top of my lungs.
Nobody answered.

I pulled myself slowly out of bed, crawling on my hands and knees to the door, my joints hurt too much to stand. I pulled myself up by the banister and slammed the door behind me in a childish huff. I looked down and there was my poor innocent mother standing at the bottom of the stairs – bewildered – with a slice of bread in her hand.

She had opened the peanut butter downstairs in the kitchen for a moment while she spread it on a piece of wheat toast.

If it wasn't the strange magnified noises and smells, it was the constant high pitch ringing in my ears. Lord forbid you put me in a room with fluorescent lights, the ringing doubled from the burning trapped screams of a thousand pins being stretched in high heat.
My eyes were no help either. The spots, they never stopped. I could no longer read, my eyes could never sit still when I tried. They darted back and forth, fluttered like

a drum roll. Even when they focused, oh… the spots.

The floaters followed me – my eyes looked like a windshield after a long drive. The spots, the smudges, the streaks from the bugs you hit along the way. I tried to draw them, but you can't look directly at them. If only I could've connected them, perhaps they would've revealed the secret of life or at least a map to a buried treasure.

My taste buds changed as well. If you couldn't tell, I was not the kind of girl who bought expensive clothes or shoes, I did not insist on fancy foods. But my newly found senses forced high tastes on a few extravagances. I could now taste chlorine and minerals in water, to a point where I found it undrinkable. I began buying expensive bottled water. I even did a blind taste test on myself to make sure I wasn't being influenced by the sleekness of the labels. I could taste the residual soap on glasses, utensils, and white rice. I began buying plastic cups, forks and spoons. I could smell chemicals in most shampoos and conditioners – most made me want to puke or runaway from my own hair. I would try to wash out the smell again – and end up exactly where I started. It was a vicious circle.

By the way, when I die, please make sure I go with the finest bottle of Bumble and Bumble Curl Conscious shampoo.

Then please, put me back out to sea.

Most brains have the ability to differentiate the important from the trivial. When you're in a loud room, your brain is capable of drowning out the chatter, allowing the insignificant to slide under the radar. Lyme disease ruins that function, leaving you with a room full of competing sounds and smells, all of equal magnitude. Lyme leaves you with superpowers nobody's ever wanted.

Everyone laughed at these symptoms, even my own mom, and I am the first to admit if I wasn't the one experiencing them I would probably find them silly, or at least harmless. But nobody gets used to bursting into tears at a department store because the manager announces something over the loudspeaker Nobody gets used to the merciless ringing in your ears, the floaters in your eyes, the ceaseless intrusions of your senses.

I saw a news story about Lyme online a few months ago, only to find it was about another patient who had committed suicide. This woman with Lyme had gone to multiple doctors begging them to make her deaf. She couldn't take the noise anymore. She couldn't deal with the broken volume knob in her head. Nobody understood the severity of her symptoms. Nobody knew how to correctly treat her and nobody would make a hearing person deaf. Now she no longer hears anything at all. I hope heaven is as quiet for her as she wished.

15 how on earth did they miss this?

I went to my first appointment with Dr. Harris the Lyme specialist in Redwood City, California. In the waiting room, I answered a list of questions to determine how many classic Lyme symptoms I had, and how severe the disease had become. This was the form:

- ☑ **Fevers**
- ☑ **Sore throats**
- ☑ **Hearing: buzzing, ringing, decreased hearing**
- ☑ **Increased motion sickness, vertigo, spinning**
- ☑ **Off balance, "tippy" feeling**
- ☑ **Light-headedness, wooziness, unavoidable need to sit or lie**
- ☑ **Tingling, numbness**
- ☑ **Burning or stabbing sensation**
- ☑ **Shooting pain**
- ☑ **Skin hypersensitivity**
- ☑ **Dental pain**
- ☑ **Neck creaks and crack, stiffness, neck pain**
- ☑ **Fatigue, tired, poor stamina**
- ☑ **Insomnia, fractionated sleep, early awakening**
- ☑ **Napping during the day**
- ☑ **Unexplained weight gain**
- ☑ **Unexplained hair loss**

- ☑ Unexplained menstrual irregularity
- ☑ Queasy stomach or nausea
- ☑ Constipation
- ☑ Diarrhea
- ☑ Bladder irritability/dysfunction
- ☑ Lower abdominal pain, cramps
- ☑ Heart palpitations or skipping
- ☑ Chest wall pain or sore ribs
- ☑ Head congestion
- ☑ Breathlessness, "air hunger" unexplained chronic cough
- ☑ Night sweats
- ☑ Persistent swollen glands
- ☑ Joint pain
- ☑ Joint swelling
- ☑ Unexplained back pain
- ☑ Stiffness of joints or back
- ☑ Muscle pain or cramps
- ☑ Obvious muscle weakness
- ☑ Twitching of the face or other muscles
- ☑ Tremors
- ☑ Headache
- ☑ Light sensitivity
- ☑ Sound sensitivity
- ☑ Vision: double, blurry, floaters
- ☑ Ear pain
- ☑ Confusion, difficult thinking
- ☑ Difficulty with concentration, reading, problem absorbing new information
- ☑ Word finding problems, name block

- ☑ **Reversing numbers/letters**
- ☑ **Difficulty Writing**
- ☑ **Forgetfulness, poor short term memory, poor attention**
- ☑ **Disorientation, getting lost, going to the wrong places**
- ☑ **Speech errors – wrong word, misspeaking**
- ☑ **Mood swings, irritability, depression**
- ☑ **Anxiety, panic attacks**
- ☑ **Psychosis (Hallucinations, delusions, paranoia, rage)**

How on *earth* did they miss this?

16 that sounds about right

I couldn't sleep. I lay on my friend Jac's couch all night at her house up in the Hollywood hills. Kayden had been gone for a few weeks now and my room was still filled with her things. Once I had gotten up off the floor the morning she left me, I lost it. I smashed a number of giant holes in my walls. I left hundreds of small bits of wood lodged in the drywall and carpet from my favorite acoustic guitar I'd smashed into pieces. I had cuts all over my hands from the wall and wood. I would have demolished the entire room if I'd had the energy.

The specialist, Dr. Stephen Harris, who I went to see in Redwood City confirmed my test results and ordered my first PICC line to be put in at Cedar Sinai Hospital in Los Angeles. A PICC, which stands for Peripherally Inserted Central Catheter is a near forty-centimeter thin tube that runs from the vein in your upper arm to the tip of your heart and stays there 24 hours a day while one is receiving medication intravenously. In two days I was going to go back to San Diego to meet with my home nurse and start my first day of treatment.

I spent the night writing. About faith. About life. About Kayden. I lay still with my eyes open, staring out the long partly open window that took up almost the entire wall of

Jac's apartment. The morning air was cool and wet, the sun was coming up over the Hollywood sign, over the top of the mountain straight across the way. It turned six a.m. Out of the corner of my eye I saw Jac had opened her door. She stood in the frame wearing a short white terrycloth robe.

"Did you sleep?" Jac asked.

"Nope."

"Surgery's tomorrow?"

"Yep."

"Want to go skydiving?" Jac asked indifferently rubbing her eyes and moving her dark brown hair off her face.

"Sure." I said evenly without turning my head. "That sounds about right."

We had once discussed going skydiving together, years earlier when we were fresh out of high school and roommates in Boston where I attended college for a whole two weeks before dropping out. Neither of us had ever mentioned it again. I put my shoes on and took my painkillers. I dragged my sore body off the couch and into Jac's car. We hit the road to Lake Elsinore, about an hour and a half away. I opened the window part way and felt the cool desert air hit my face.

"Any word from Kayden?"

"Nothing."

"I think we should just refer to her as *Saint Kayden* from now on, her good will simply knows no bounds."

I laughed.

"My mom was sweet enough to offer to pack up her stuff for me. I can't do it."

"You should just set that bitch's shit on fire."

Jac squeezed my hand and I looked back out the window. We pulled up to the skydiving office and signed the paperwork accepting that we were responsible for any injury or death that may occur. The instructor took one look at me and pulled me into another room.

"I want you to know we have a lot people come here who are ill, people who have cancer, people who can't walk. You're in good hands," he assured me kindly.

"Thank you."

"A lot of people find this very life affirming."

I smiled at the notion then said, "…I just think it's time to go."

The instructor furrowed his eyebrows a bit confused; I nodded my chin towards the clock on the wall and smiled softly.

I didn't feel trapped in the plane this time. Maybe because the door was already wide open from take off till - I can only assume – landing.

I walked to the edge of the door; my foot landed flat halfway between the ledge and the sky. I pressed one knee down against the hard metal floor of the plane. I kneeled, as if awaiting my coronation. I bent my other knee over the edge of the heavens in anticipation of the crown.

I looked down. Thirteen thousand feet; between me and the rest of my world, between me and whatever I was about to endure.

I knew I could die.

I knew I might die soon anyway.

I looked down those thirteen thousand feet and I thought for a moment about Kayden's eyes as I kissed her goodbye the last time before she drove away. I thought about Jen asleep in the bed next to me and Eric passed out in the other room as I walked down the hallway in the middle of the night carrying a backpack full of clothes. I thought about Sara holding my hand as I lay my head in her lap on the subway.

I needed freedom – the type of freedom only death, in one form or another, can bring. I did not want a slow death. I wanted the fastest way to a rebirth. I wanted to jump out of that plane, break through the earth and burst out of the ocean on the other side of the world, clean.

Purified. Exempt.

It was an active step in a world where the passivity of pain had swelled so heavily I had almost drowned. I was finally in control. If I lost whatever else I had left to lose in that moment, it was my choice, it was on me.

I felt my instructor put his hands on my shoulders, his clips attached to my back and side. He yelled over the wind in what felt like the quietest of whispers.

"ARE YOU READY?!"

I stared down at the great empty earth.

"No." I said.

And jumped.

I fell in perfect peace at a hundred and twenty miles per hour through the air. Minutes later my parachute opened and we drifted through a clear blue sky. I wanted to stay up there forever – where nothing could touch me, nothing could box me in, nothing could be asked of me again. I was as irrelevant as a balloon that had slipped out of a birthday boy's hand.

I watched as another pair fell from the plane above. At the time they were supposed to open their parachute, they went spinning into quick circles through the air.

"Oh shit, they're chute didn't open," my instructor told me – no longer having to yell. It was so quiet up there; there was a stillness in falling I had never experienced nor expected.

"Is that Jac?!" I asked back.

"Yep." He said.

They spun out of control for almost a minute before they finally got the second chute open and began gliding slowly down to earth. Jac later told me her instructor was on her back screaming "FUCK!!!" the whole time which was less than comforting for her.

I'm sorry she had to experience that but I sure as hell am glad that by the slim luck of the draw I got paired with the gorgeous Australian instructor with the nice tattoos and working chute instead of the stubby guy with the lame pack and the low threshold for fear.

I rolled onto the dirt. My ribs ached from the impact of the world. I felt the beginning, the shift, the first step of true abandonment had occurred.

I bought a bottle of water and a single package of brown sugar pop tarts at the gas station and fell asleep on the drive home. I slept in soreness through the night on Jac's couch and awoke prepared to walk through the doors of the hospital. I was ready to begin the first day of the rest of my life.

• • • • •

I'd never had a PICC line before, I hadn't even heard of one, so I didn't know what to expect. I thought it was something simple, like one of the thousands of IVs I received at the hospital.

I was laid out on a gurney in a sterile white and grey room. Next thing I knew I was surrounded by six men and women in blue gowns, scrub caps, masks, and gloves. At least four of them were interns but I couldn't tell which since they all looked like baby blue clones.

"Okay, here we go," Clone A smiled at me through his mask as Clone B stuck a long needle full of Lidocaine into the inside of my upper left arm which soon became numb.

I felt the tube slide into my arm. I felt it climb up as the nerves around my heart twitched and jumped at the intrusion. Clone B explained they were going to flush the line. The saline was pushed, my veins tightened up. I felt as if I couldn't breathe.

"You okay?" Clone C asked. I had turned bright red and then pale white. The shock of the flush was greater on my body than I had imagined.

"*I felt that in my neck.*" I whispered.

"What?"

The clones stopped moving.

"It was in my neck." I repeated a little louder, pointing with my right hand to the left side of my neck.

I watched them look at each other.

"I'm sorry sweetie, were going to have to do it again," they apologized. One of the clones went into an analogy about my veins, explaining they were like highway 5 splitting into the 405 and the 405 to the 101. Every once in awhile, when threading the tube, it tries to take a detour. In this case, the detour was my neck.

I felt it as they pulled the tube out through my arm and began threading it again. My chest tightened once more at the saline's release, my face went red, I caught my breath.

I was helped up a few minutes later – my treatment ready to begin.

17

there's 100 in a box,
so 3 boxes...
the answer is 3 boxes

Dr. Steven Harris, my specialist, had set up my care back home in San Diego with a home nurse. Dr. Harris was what I would call dreamy and if you haven't guessed by now, I am not one to ever use the word dreamy. He is a young savant with thick brunette hair, deep golden brown eyes and a sweet smile. He was the first doctor to really look into my eyes, not just at them.

"Wow…" he said compassionately, when he first looked at me. "You are in so much pain aren't you?"

He held my hand when he helped me off the table.

He was kind.

I felt saved.

Dr. Harris had me try to walk a straight line during my first visit. In all the tens of thousands of dollars worth of high tech tests people had performed on me, nobody had ever asked me to do something as simple as walk for them.

I tried. I took a step and fell down.

He had me close my eyes and try to stand on one foot.

I tried. I fell down again.

He had me try again, this time with my eyes open.

No luck.

~ there's 100 in a box so 3 boxes, the answer is 3 boxes ~

He diagnosed my vertigo in a matter of minutes, something nobody else had even noticed

Dr. Harris was the first doctor to meet me with empathy instead of suspicion, with assurance instead of judgment or doubt. He was the first doctor who had a plan, who could finish my sentences because he knew the disease better than anyone. He finally took the burden of proof off of me – removed the largest load I had ever carried upon my back and trashed it.

All I had to do now was fight.

Dr. Harris and I have a very similar sense of humor, one that continues to confuse every other doctor and intern who has sat in on our appointments.

We went over the medications I was to be started on. I told him I couldn't take a particular supplement since it was made with fish oil.

"What about this one?" He asked straight faced, "It's made out of crushed dead baby squirrel brains, that's cool right? "

"Oh yeah, that's totally fine with me," I responded without cracking a smile, "I only care about fish, fuck squirrels."

We tried to read each other, then broke, laughing.

"I also need you to take this medication," he said pretending to write down notes on his pad, "but it's made out of panda fetus."

I began my first IV treatment at home in my room. The nurse stood guard with an epi-pen in case anything went wrong. I started S.A.S.H. Saline. Antibiotics. Saline. Heparin.

The strength of the medicine knocked me out. I swallowed my first handful of oral antibiotics and anti-virals for the co-infections and the pills that would keep my gallbladder from crystallizing, a side effect of the harsh treatments I was now beginning.

I believed treatment would be the easy part, and in one way it was. There is nothing more difficult than battling a shadow. Now it had a name.

But when you push, Lyme pushes back. And when you try to kill Lyme, Lyme fights back harder to kill you.

Now I knew my enemy.
And my enemy was ready for war.

New symptoms that had slowly been seeping in were now becoming much worse. The first was speaking. I'm not sure which came first, the difficulty in the act of talking, or the inability to remember how. The fatigue became so overwhelming that for days, sometimes weeks on end, I had no energy to form words. Forcing sounds out of my mouth felt like the most arduous task in the world. When I did try to speak, I was told to repeat myself because nobody could hear me. Being forced to say something twice could bring me to tears.

My mom taught herself how to text message because it was impossible for me to hold a conversation. She would sit at the edge of my bed and I would scribble down nearly illegible notes to her with a pen I kept near my pillow.

It was no longer just the act of speaking but remembering how to speak that was waning. I could no longer remember who my professors had been back at school, what someone said to me, why I was in a room. I no longer remembered places I had been, childhood memories I was supposed to have, people I was supposed to know. Perhaps most frustrating, I could no longer remember the names of things around me. I'd use hand gestures over and over again to try to get across what I was saying until someone figured it out. I couldn't remember words like carpool, cup, folder, dresser, D.N.A.; but I could still draw a double helix. I'd get more and more aggravated trying to get my point across or asking for something I needed. My sentences were all broken. I began to develop a stutter while my brain backfired, started up and stalled again, tirelessly pushing the engine to turn over.

My memory got so bad that my mom bought a Winnie the Pooh memory board game for three-year-olds and tried to practice basic skills with me. I couldn't even do that. I would find one Tigger, flip the tile back over and not only forget where it was but what game I was supposed to be playing.

I had always been punished for my memory. My closest friends used to say it was my greatest blessing and my greatest curse. I was relieved when it went away…
Part of me wishes it never came back.

Over the years I learned to lie to people about my memory. For instance, I once ran into a girl at the dog park who I had spoken to once for a couple of minutes a year before. She came up to me to ask about my dog, having no recollection of ever seeing either of us before. I remembered where she worked, where she was from, which dog was hers, that her dog's name was Tony, that she named him after Tony Gwynn because she was a big fan of the Padres. But I didn't say a word.

Losing my memory was freeing. People always got the wrong idea when I told them what I knew, what I remembered. They never looked at me the same. They always thought it was on purpose, that it was personal or that I cared more than I did… that I was using my memory against them. But it was never something I controlled. When it came back I made a decision: I would never again feel ashamed for knowing what I know, I would never apologize for my memory *ever* again.

My brain wasn't the only thing that was being given a beating. The pain was now so bad I could no longer get up or down stairs if I wasn't crawling on my hands and knees. Many days I had to get to the bathroom the same way, pulling myself up by the toilet seat. Some days the fatigue was so massive that I couldn't get there at all. I'd have to pee into a trash bag and stuff it with old towels and junk, praying nobody would notice.

I'll never forget the first delusional episode that happened after I was diagnosed. I was trying to move my desk over a few inches when I all of a sudden felt the whole room spin. I had exerted too much energy and blacked out.

The next thing I knew, I was sitting down on my chair but I had no idea where I was; what room I was in, what city, what house. I didn't recognize a thing. And I remember, for the first time, this sudden state of delirium didn't send me into a panic. I recognized it, I observed it, and I waited for it to pass. I knew its source. I could finally rationalize what had once been so overwhelmingly irrational. It was an indescribable relief.

With my intensive treatment and my disabilities multiplied, I began living in my ten foot by ten foot room full time. I was going stir-crazy. My mom saw the giant holes in my wall and let me keep going. My brother helped me destroy the dividing wall between his old room and mine. I put all my instruments into the new room, turning it into a makeshift studio. I hoped someday I would have enough strength to record music again.

My mom later explained that she actually let me break down the wall after she found me collapsed at the bottom of the stairs.

I don't remember. I guess I fell down.

I painted my formerly blue walls red and black. I didn't want to be reminded of Kayden everyday, plus, I needed to see something more powerful when I opened my eyes. This was war.

Kayden and I hadn't spoken since she'd left, then one day out of nowhere, she called.

Months had passed and my curiosity for closure got the best of me. I answered the phone. I was hoping I would finally get an explanation for why she did what she did. It turned out she was just calling to brag that she got into a master's program to become a psychologist.

Yes ladies and gentleman… a *psychologist.*

"So have you gotten help?" I asked her. "Have you talked to someone?"

Nope.

"You're going into psychology but you haven't talked to anyone about your suicide attempts? About your eating disorder? Your childhood? The rape? About, I don't know, the fact that you once literally put a loaded gun into your mouth?"

Nope.

"Huh…" I continued, "Well was there anything else you wanted to tell me? Do you finally know why you took off? How you were able to just leave me like that?"

Nope. Nothing.

I told her I finally understood why so many people she knew beat the shit out of her.

I only talked to Kayden one more time via text message. She owed my mom money for the cost of shipping all her things back to Pennsylvania but refused to send it. I figured the easiest thing to do was threaten to tell her parents everything I knew about her life. I threatened to tell them everything if I didn't get the money within two weeks. I got the check in one.

~ there's 100 in a box so 3 boxes, the answer is 3 boxes ~

It's a good lesson to everyone. As the great Roseanne Conner once said:

Use me and I'll set you on fire, you bastard.

• • • • •

I finished a month of IV antibiotics, had my first PICC line removed and was put on a combination of oral medications.

It was nice to finally take a real shower again without having my arm with the PICC wrapped up in massive amounts of Saran wrap.

A number of people had slipped away throughout the year and a half of my being ill, and now that I was diagnosed, I began to watch how the few who stuck around reacted.

One of my cousins and his family had stayed away from me since I'd been back in California and even after I was diagnosed, they wouldn't see me because they believed I was contagious. That's one of the things that sucks about having a critical, potentially fatal illness that nobody knows anything about. And in case you were wondering, no… Lyme disease is *not* contagious.

Another one of my cousins, Randy, a professional scuba diver, brought down her equipment after my PICC was removed. She hooked me up to the oxygen tank and helped me into the pool in our backyard. I lay at the bottom looking up at the sun pushing its way through the water. I fell asleep in the pool underwater on the cement floor. I had grown up spending as much time as possible underwater. I used to set up elaborate forts on the top of the pool and hide in there for hours. Nothing could hurt me there.

My brother Stephen had an unconventional way of dealing with my illness as well. He had just finished playing the original Shrek for the reading and workshop of the show on Broadway. It should go without saying how insanely talented he is, as an actor, as a singer, and by the spring of 2008, as a hilarious stand up comic. By the time I'm telling you this story, you probably know my brother best from Nickelodeon – for Gustavo Rock on *Big Time Rush*, but at the time he was all over the comedy scene.

My brother and his best friend Sahba dragged me out of the house every month or two to take me to a comedy club. I was helped out to Sahba's car, then into the bar, then into a seat up front where I could forget for a little while what was happening and just laugh – I'd laugh when the comics were funny, I laughed even harder when they weren't. Real crickets terrify me; awkward metaphorical ones are absolutely hilarious. One night, in the car on the way to a show my brother was headlining at the Miramar marine base, he asked if I wanted to go up on stage.

I was on a decent amount of medication, enough that with the unrecommended combination of a couple of beers at the club, I said yes.

I had talked about trying stand up someday but never really planned on it. I performed my first set that night, sitting on a stool, in front of four hundred Marines.

I felt free up there. It had been so long since I'd been on stage. I just started to talk.

~ there's 100 in a box so 3 boxes, the answer is 3 boxes ~

I talked about my illness, talked about my sore throats and how since I spent so much time alone I had learned to play games with myself, like:

How many otter pops does it take to get diabetes?

I made jokes about how, with my luck, I got the one critical illness that *doesn't* make you skinny.

I decided I'd try pushing the boundaries a little to see what would happen so I talked about my dislike of rape whistles.

"Nobody likes the sound of a whistle," I told them. "Nobody comes running to you when you blow a whistle; they just have flashbacks of seventh grade P.E. and run the other way."

"What we need is a rape violin," I continued. "Everyone loves to stop to hear a violin. Plus the rapist himself might take a step back and think, 'hey wait a minute, this girl can really play the violin… *tremendous*.'"

I talked to about a hundred marines that night after the show. I don't know if it was my brother's intention but he made me feel part of a team again. Whenever I sat in the greenroom with him and went up on stage at another club, I was part of that group of performers and was always treated as such. I stopped suffering for a moment…

I just laughed.

18 july 4th, 2008

By the summer of 2008, I finally felt like we were starting to get on top of everything. But July 4th was approaching, I should have known doom was waiting just around the bend.

July 4th, 2008 my mom got a call from her sister in Montreal. We needed to get out there right away. My mom, my brother, and I tried to find a flight out but it was impossible to find anything last minute on a holiday weekend. Plus, we would have had to find a last minute dog sitter for Junior and Omega. My Granddad was sick and had taken a turn for the worse so we wasted no time. We packed up the motorhome and as soon as the sun went down, we hit the road.

· · · · ·

My Granddad Harry, was my only Grandfather. But over the years he had become much more.

I was only nine years old when my biological father walked out for the last time. It was Thanksgiving. *White Men Can't Jump* was on TV, leftover Kentucky Fried Chicken had begun to stale in open styrofoam containers that were spread out on the kitchen table. He was there, and then he was gone.

It was a loss in a conceptual sense – to no longer have *a* father was difficult. But losing *my* father was not much of a loss at all. He was not a good man. It wasn't hard to see him go.

When I was eighteen years old my grandmother, Gloria passed away, leaving my grandfather alone for the first time in sixty years. My grandma meant the world to me. She was a musical prodigy. She could play any song by ear. It is said that she once broke glass with her voice. She sang and the world stopped. She would calm her nerves with a sip or two of cough syrup before she'd sit down at the piano and blow people away. She sang side by side on the bench with me. She went into the recording studio with me the summer before she passed away. She, in many ways, taught me how to play.

When my grandma laughed, no sound came out, just a wheezing contagious air and tears that streamed slowly from her light green eyes to the corners of an open mouth.

My grandfather was the quiet support in the relationship. They had met at sixteen, were married at seventeen. They were the couple that made us all believe in love. Neither had ever even slept with another. Neither had even looked at another besides Julia Roberts for him and Robert Redford for her. My heart broke when she passed away, all our hearts broke for at least a moment. She was the matriarch. She was the joy.

At her funeral, I sat on a small couch and held my Granddad's hand while everyone came up one by one to give him their condolences. As they closed the casket he kissed her goodbye while the Rabbi pulled him off, sobbing, praying that kiss was going to bring her back to life. Nobody thought he would last even six months without her.

Only a few months after her passing, sitting in the back of a required English class in Boston during my first week of college, I wrote a pro/con list. By the end of the hour I decided I had more important places to be. I packed up my books. I went to the admissions office and returned my twenty six thousand dollar scholarship after being asked if I was serious by the administrator *three* times.

I heard the thunder applaud as I opened the heavy double doors. I ran to my car as it began to pour rain and scraped my permit off the back window. I returned to the office with a handful of soaking wet pieces of a sticker and got my money back for my parking space. I ran, dripping, to White Hall, up the spiral stairs to the fourth floor, to my cramped dorm room. I had forgotten my keys. I banged on the door till my knuckles began to bleed, 'til Jac finally woke up and opened it. I gathered my instruments. I gathered my clothes. I gathered everything I owned and kissed my friends goodbye. I got in my car and hit the road north to Montreal.

I dialed my cell phone, "Meet me at Picassos Papa," I said. "I'm going to buy you a number 3 (a stack of small blueberry pancakes) and a cup of coffee. If you'll take me, I'm moving in."

• • • • •

I held onto the wheel of the motorhome, watching the road as the fireworks broke overhead; the fourth of July celebration had begun. My mom, brother, and I had hit the fifteen north towards Las Vegas. We had no plans to stop, no plans to camp, no plans to play. We needed to get to Montreal as fast as the motorhome would take us. Dad had been sick for a while, he had hit rough patches before and made it, but we needed to get there to make sure he was okay. I had just taken over the wheel. Radiohead's "In Rainbows" had just started spinning, it could hypnotize me for the next hour as the lights of the cars slipped by on either side and the white dotted lines swirled into a stream.

CRACK!!!

The lights exploded around us. Omega hid under the passenger seat. She hated loud noises. Junior, having lived with me in New York City, couldn't have cared less.

BOOM!!!

"Fuck!" I yelled and hit the power button to turn off the stereo. That wasn't the fireworks. The tire blew. I held on tightly to the steering wheel as the remaining tires wobbled and slowed to a crawl. Quickly veering to the right I found the nearest exit ramp and pulled over. We'd had the motorhome checked out at the dealer before we left.

Somehow they had missed this.

We waited for four hours at the truck stop. The sun was coming up. The desert air still cold. I laid in the back of the camper with my eyes closed, the clock was ticking, we didn't have time for this at all.

"Everything's set." The mechanic told us, handing us back the heavy set of keys.

"Are you sure you checked the rest of the tires?" My mom asked respectfully. "We can't afford to have another blow-out."

"Yes ma'am, you're good to go."

We still had nearly three thousand miles ahead of us. We had hardly made a dent in the map, we would just have to try harder. My brother took over for a couple hours, blasting musical theatre numbers from the stereo, singing along to the soundtracks of Annie and Avenue Q. We all had our genres that rotated with the drivers seat. My brother – one of the rare straight men fresh off Broadway - played musicals. My mom played The Beatles, Herman's Hermits, and The Animals. I played R.E.M., the Dixie Chicks, Jackson 5, Iron and Wine. We listened to whatever would keep us going. We hit Utah.

I used to love driving through Utah. Bryce Canyon. High pillars of sand that stood so still your heartbeat bounced off the walls and echoed loudly back to you. Small hidden off-the-highway towns. Turquoise jewelry and shotguns sold at "Indian" stores connected to gas stations. There was no time for that. We would sleep in shifts while the other one drove. It was my turn again. I had rested awhile and I wanted to seize my energy since it so sporadically came about. I turned on an old Stone Temple Pilots CD.

BOOM!!!

"Are you fucking kidding me?!" I yelled back to my mom who had just lay down to get some sleep. I hadn't even been driving ten minutes. The whole motor home shook. I pulled over to the side of the highway. My mom jumped out of the side door and returned a moment later shaking her head.

"We blew another one," she said in disbelief. "Call triple A again."

· · · · ·

Nobody had touched the piano since my Grandma had passed away. My first day after moving in, I sat at the bench and ran my fingers lightly over the keys. I could feel my Grandma's hands next to mine, could sense her soft green terrycloth robe brush against my arm, smell her White Shoulder perfume, her head resting against mine. I began pushing the keys down one by one, I plucked out *Somewhere Over The Rainbow,* and could hear her sing. The piano missed her. We all missed her. My Grandpa missed her in a way that, in this lifetime, I may never know.

I put up teenage posters on my new pastel flower wall papered room: Tori Amos, Salvador Dali, Radiohead. I covered the peach carpet with a fake fur rug, lined the dresser with my collection of DVDs and books.

I followed my Grandpa's routine.

I woke up early every morning and baked fresh blueberry bran muffins for him or poured us each a bowl of Cheerios, whichever he preferred. I took out his chart and kept track of his insulin and blood sugar levels. We ate side by side every morning as we watched *The Price is Right* on the small TV in the kitchen. My Grandmother had loved the show too. She became what some would call "overly invested" in the plight of each contestant, often crying when someone won a washer and dryer combo, or soup for a year.

For most of my life, the closest thing I had to a dad was Dan Conner on reruns of *Roseanne*. I used to think about a life where he and I would fix motorcycles together in the garage, that he'd teach me how to play poker, that I could feel safe knowing that if anyone ever hurt me he wouldn't hesitate to beat the crap out of them. When I moved in with my grandfather, I thought the greatest thing that could happen would be I would get to know him better. But instead I got the one thing I never thought I'd have outside of TV land… I got a dad.

We spent everyday together, going to the movies, walking at the mall, going to dinner. Everyday I'd help him with his jacket and scarf, check his bag to make sure he had some candies and half a tuna fish or chopped egg sandwich, something to keep his blood sugar even during dialysis. I'd often meet him at St. Mary's Hospital to keep him company during part of his treatment. We'd sit with split earphones and watch daytime movies on a miniature television.

I'd brush Dad's hair while he sat on the kitchen chair and ate his breakfast. Sometimes I'd make his hair into a faux hawk for the hell of it or give him my corduroy cowboy hat to wear, anything to see that deep dimpled Walter Matthau smile. He and my grandma had a huge California King bed, so I often lay in his room with him watching old John Wayne movies or *Dancing with the Stars*.

Every night Dad would fall asleep holding my hand. If I let go he'd wake up, so I would grab his hand again and he'd fall back to sleep. Sometimes I'd wait there for hours, holding his hand, just so as not to wake him.

My grandfather became the dad I'd always needed. He loved and supported me. He embodied loyalty and responsibility. He treated me like a lady.

I brought as much life as I could back into his house. I became extremely protective of him and that instinct was returned. Protection was the number one thing I always imagined having from a dad when I was growing up. Even when he was stuck in the hospital, laid up post surgery, he would insist that he was there to look out for me, that nobody better mess with me or they would answer to him.

He fought through every battle set before him while never forgetting to take time to wink at the nurses. When I moved to New York City, I came up to Montreal to see him at least seven times a year. We spoke on the phone four to five days a week without fail.

• • • • •

BOOM!

It wasn't possible.

A third tire blew while I was behind the wheel. The second one had been replaced miles back. All of the tires were checked and again guaranteed to be fine.

By the time we got back on the road we were only in Wyoming. It had been three days and we hadn't even passed into the central time zone. The summer sun shone down against the R.V., heating up the metal walls like a toaster oven.

"Did you turn on the generator?!" My mom yelled back to me while she drove.

"Yeah, the air conditioning won't turn on!" I answered, pushing the starter again.

It was over ninety degrees outside. There was no way we could live in there with no air, especially with the dogs, especially with me as sick as I was. I still had fevers. I needed sleep to heal. I couldn't sleep in that heat. My mom and brother felt the same way, there was no choice, we had to stop and get it fixed. My mom found a repair shop who promised they would have us out of there in a day. It took them three. We stayed in a motel off the highway while the R.V. was at the shop, antsy and frustrated, we waited in the middle of nowhere.

"Dad, hang in there okay? We are on our way," I told him.

He was weak, I had never heard him sound so defeated. But he had pulled through before when nobody ever expected him to. He had beat cancer. He had survived two leg amputations and learned how to *walk* again. He had been pushed hard and *always* pulled through.

We hit the road again. The air conditioner held steady, we could all breathe. The tires rolled firm, we were doing good, we were on our way. The trip was harder on me than I thought it would be. The constant trembling of the road exacerbated the nausea I could never shake. I felt as if I never slept. The side effects from my medications were worsened by the sight of constant movement, of blurs of trees and buildings that flew by in a rage past the windows.

"Okay, I'm ready to drive again, what's the chance of a fourth tire blowing right?" I told my mom and brother. We were all very much aware that almost every bad thing that had happened thus far on the trip had happened while I drove, but they were exhausted and knew I could get us at least a few inches off the map.

It was eleven at night. No explosions. So far so good, I thought. I watched as the flashing orange lights and approaching rows of cones signaled construction ahead. Speed limit: 65 miles per hour. Construction started, I winded the motor home into the single lane that hugged a cement median. I could feel the un-brushed breath of a trucker passing. The speed limit changed: 25 miles per hour. Detour ahead.

We were crossing the state line. Construction ended. I took the R.V. back up to 65.

Then came the sirens

There comes a point when the words "you got to be kidding me" just don't cut it anymore. I pulled over the motorhome on the side of the highway. The officer cautiously approached the passenger window.

"Excuse me miss, do you realize how fast you were going?"

"Yes sir," I told him. "I believe I was going sixty-five, the construction zone was over so I went back to the speed limit I saw before it started."

"The speed limit here is *fifty-five*. Where are you are heading?"

"Montreal, it's a family emergency," I explained.

He paused.

"Can you please step out of the vehicle miss?"

"Wait, where are you going with her?" My mom interrupted.

"Just over to the patrol car, now please stay seated where you are."

I assured my mom it was okay and opened the side door. I followed him over to the highway patrol car praying he wouldn't make me walk a straight line since it was still something I couldn't do.

"Get in please," he said.

"Excuse me?" I hadn't done anything.

"You can sit in the front seat," he said. "There are too many cars on the road tonight, it isn't safe to stand out here."

I looked around at the deserted Iowa highway. I opened the passenger door and sat down. The screens and cameras flashed with impatience, lit the inside of the black and white car up with a green hue.

"Where did you say you were going?" He asked again.

"Montreal."

"Are you an American citizen miss?"

"No sir, I'm Canadian, but we're legal residents."

He asked for my passport and green card. He wasn't a border patrol agent, what the hell did he need with all this? I saw the reflection of blue and white lights flashing from the windshield. Another cop car had pulled up behind us while my name, social security number, license and address were typed into his space age computer on the dashboard. The other cop approached the passenger window and I rolled it down.

"Hi." I said smiling.

This was hilarious. My eye line was at his waist, I noticed the gun on his belt and ran through a *Requiem for a Dream* opportunity in my head.

"Anything I can help with sir?" He asked looking past me.

"We have a suspicious vehicle here, could be an attempt to flee the country," he responded.

"What?" I interrupted.

Before he could answer he noticed the same thing I did. My mom had not stayed seated. She was extremely concerned, not understanding why this strange man had taken me into his car alone. I was obviously the youngest person in the vehicle, I was anything but in charge. Fifteen plus minutes had already passed and she was getting impatient. She had opened the window on the side of the R.V., had stuck half her torso and head out and was staring at the three of us.

"MA'AM, GET BACK IN THE VEHICLE!" The officer announced over the loud speaker.

"WHAT'S GOING ON?!" My mom yelled back at the cops waiving her hands.

"MA'AM," he repeated even more sternly than before, "I SAID GET BACK IN THE VEHICLE. DO NOT PUT YOUR HEAD OUT THE WINDOW OR STEP OUT OF THE VEHICLE IN ANY WAY AGAIN."

I brought my hand up to my neck. "Cut it out!" I mouthed silently at my mom trying not to laugh. She was going to get us killed.

She retreated back into the motor home but five minutes later had pressed her face against the back window trying to see what was going on. I found this funny, he didn't. He got out of the car and scolded her. I was alone. I thought about all the things I could do. The keys were in the ignition, I could go for a ride. I could run the cops over. I could tell jokes over the loud speaker. I sat quietly.

He made multiple phone calls when he got back. He checked up on my license, my identity, my record or lack there of. I still have no idea what he thought we were trying to run from. It was Iowa, maybe he thought we were trying to flee the scene of an imaginary baseball game played by ghosts. Maybe he thought he had stumbled upon a case that if he could just crack he would be promoted. Maybe he kept me waiting there in that car for over forty-five fucking minutes while he pictured the headlines:

Highway Patrolman pulls over girl for driving less than ten miles over the speed limit only to find family and dogs in conspiracy to flee the country!

(Apparently his imagination also had newspapers with extra long headlines.) The picture on the cover would be of him shaking hands with the governor of Iowa, no, the president of the United States and the prime minister of Canada who would congratulate him, "Thanks for keeping these *scoundrels* out of our country!"

"Yes well done!" the president would agree, "anyone else would have thought this was nothing more than a family heading home because a loved one was sick but not you! No, you were clever enough to see through their sly cover." And then all three of the men would start to make out with each other.

Don't ask me, it wasn't my fantasy.

Nearly an hour later, the second cop car finally went on its way and the highway patrolman let me out of the car without even a ticket. My mom hugged me tightly when I opened the metal door and climbed back into the cramped R.V. I was exhausted from the whole ordeal. We all were. There is nothing like being stuck in a cop car to put a kink in that long distance driving mentality. We found a campground nearby that we could plug in at. We would start driving again at sunrise, which was now only a few hours away.

The next two days we did nothing but drive. Well, my brother and mom did nothing but drive, I was banned. I lay on the kitchen table turned bed with Junior and watched my reruns with my headphones on. Finally we were only twenty minutes from the border! From there we were a mere 6-7 hours away from dad. We were going to make it! After three blown tires, a broken air conditioner, and a run in with the highway patrol we were now only twenty minutes from Canada, from our homeland.

"Let's get gas before we get to customs," my mom said. We had lied so many times going over the border when my brother and I were kids that the fear of crossing had become innate, as had the tradition of stopping to get our stories straight before we got to customs. Even though we were now legal and had been for quite some time, we still always took a moment to stop and make sure we had all our green cards, passports, and papers organized. My brother pulled off the highway.

The phone rang.

"Hey dad! We made it to the border, we're almost there!" My mom answered.

She went silent.

"No," she said quietly. I looked over at her just as her face dropped. She put down the phone and without a word looked at my face in question and shook her head.

"WHAT?!" I yelled.

"No! Are you serious!?" My brother shouted from the drivers seat. After that I can only remember screaming. Loud cries overwhelmed with unadulterated pain. A hundred square feet enclosed with this sound of wailing, of horrible loss. I am not sure whether the sounds came from my mouth or theirs. But the sound was everywhere.

I felt as if the blood had all but left my heart.

You can never forget the moment you find out you have lost someone. It is like a scratch across your own existence, leaving a dent that the needle of the record player gets stuck on and repeats over and over again in your head. There are great moments in life when time slows, but in these moments of loss, time stops all together. It is a moment that divides the world into that which existed before and that which will always exist after. There is a shift in the universe – it is instant… effortless. Sometimes it shifts your world a little, sometimes it is a shift too great to bear.

Everything became dark.
And quiet.

The engine started silently, no music played as I took over the wheel and drove us slowly over the border.

We hit London, the town where my brother and I were born. It now felt like the only place I knew. The only place I wanted to be.

There was nothing left to rush for, no reason to race to Montreal, he was gone. That highway we were chasing now only pointed in one direction – the funeral.

We couldn't take that road. We couldn't go back. We did anything to delay saying goodbye and validating the inevitable.

Nobody said a word.

We checked ourselves into a hotel. We couldn't be together at that moment. The grief was too great, too individual to share such a small space.

We waited in London for three days. Asleep. Dazed. I walked through my original hometown, eyes swollen and glazed over, letting the stillness sink into me.

We arrived in Montreal. It didn't look the way it used to. It was cold now. Heartless. I spoke at the funeral. I slipped a note into Dad's jacket pocket while his body lay in the casket. I'd written the same note he once slipped into my jacket years before, the simple note I'd carried everyday with me since.

"I love you."

I grieved for my loss, and for the loss my mom felt, a loss I will never know.

My dad understood over the past two years how tough it was to be sick. We would laugh at not knowing what day it was, or month, or year. He understood how frustrating it was to be dependent; when you're a warrior at heart but now need help to even eat a meal, take a shower, walk across the room. The last time we saw each other, I had tremors in my hands as bad as his .We sat next to each other, our hands shaking in unison, competing over how much soup we could keep on the spoon. On the many nights I couldn't sleep I would wait till four a.m. my time, till it was seven his time, and call to wish him good morning. I would wish him a happy non-dialysis two day break every Saturday evening and he would always laugh. We'd laugh at anything that could get us through the day.

Somedays when we spoke, we were both too sad to say much at all. Too tired. Too sick. I would annoyingly tell him to hold a smile with me even if it killed both of us... and I would wait and count to ten through my teeth, forcing smiles on our faces as fake and wide as we could until they became real, even if just for a moment.

Dad was always a rational man, a realist, once even told me he liked to plan everything out at least ten years in advance. He loved that I was pursuing higher education, he always wore his Columbia University light blue jacket and Columbia grey beanie with pride.

But the last time I saw him, he sat with me at the piano and told me to play music.

"Forget everything else," he said "School will always be there, but you are meant to play music. Don't worry about anything else. Go play."

I was too sick after the funeral to go to the burial. Plus, I wanted to be alone. I would say my goodbyes on my time, alone with him, maybe in my dreams. I didn't know much but I knew the man in the casket wasn't him, it was just a body. Handsome Harry was off with his beautiful Gloria dancing in each others arms again.

An old friend drove me back to the RV parked outside his old home, our old home. I watched through the window in the back as family went in and out of the house. I stepped in once, only to hear screaming between my cousin and uncle, arguing about what to do with dad's prized coin collection. I couldn't be there. I turned right back out the door and climbed back into the motor home. I glued myself to my miniature DVD player. I took my medication. I didn't move.

My brother and my mom joined me forty-eight hours later. We turned on the engine, turned around, and went home.

My dad was gone. My friend. My anchor.

We drove away, and I watched as it broke from a rope that fell leisurely to the floor of the sea.

I watched out the back window as the water got murkier – as my anchor of strong and shining steel grew dim and distant, dark and blurry, as I floated away.

Not a tire blew. Not an appliance broke. Not a cop pulled us over.

Around Tennessee my friend Kristin called asking if I wanted backstage passes to Stone Temple Pilots that weekend, to a show back in San Diego.

"Thank you for thinking of me," I said. "Not this time."

19 the freaky friday - friday freaked

I'm not sure whether it was fate, or just the result of two fools who both accidentally wished on crashing planes they mistook for falling stars... but my mom was the only person I knew who understood how sick I felt.

On my thirteenth birthday, my mom pulled over on La Costa Blvd. after I asked her for the truth.

"Something is going on," I told her, "I know you and I know something is wrong. What are you hiding from me?"

She pulled the car over.

The rest I blocked out.

I was later informed that it was there she told me that the spot she had on the back of her leg had turned out to be malignant, and that even though it was removed it had already spread through her body. She told me she now had third stage melanoma in her lymph system.

My mom was hospitalized shortly after. She underwent multiple surgeries, radiation, Chemo, Interfuron and Interlukon – IL2.

She was given six months to live.

I watched as she lost her hair, as she transformed from my healthy mom to a fragile twig. She was hospitalized for months at a time. Parents in the carpool would take me to school at around six in the morning then I would be taken to the hospital at around two in the afternoon where I'd stay till at least ten at night.

My mom really couldn't talk much, she was hooked up to machines, she was drugged for the pain, she would sleep. She weighed about ninety pounds. It was too hard to always stay in the room and watch her fade away so I would sit by myself in the little lobby down the hall in a single chair that faced the communal cancer ward TV. I watched *Beverly Hills 90210* from four p.m. till six p.m. everyday on FX. I fell asleep every night in an empty house to *Roseanne*.

She survived the six-month deadline but continued to worsen and disintegrate as the next year came and went. My father's leaving had been extremely hard for her, they had been together since they were fourteen, they had been married for twenty-three years. He never came by the entire time she was dying. He never came back to see if she was okay. He performed no penance. Never even sent a card.

One day the doctor pulled me and my brother aside, told us to prepare ourselves, told us go in and say our goodbyes; that our mom wasn't going to make it through the night.

I couldn't do it.

I stood outside the room in the doorway, ready to kill. I waited for someone to tell me how to stop it. I would have sold my soul to see her well again.

To the astonishment of all her doctors, she made it

through that night. She had been part of an experimental treatment on top of radiation where she was injected with another person's tumor in the hopes that her body would recognize it as a foreign intrusion and begin fighting it – in turn fighting her own cancer that her body was ignoring. They had tried this four times already. The morning after we were told to say goodbye, the fifth tumor worked. Her body was fighting the cancer.

We lived in that hospital for nearly three years.

I had taken care of her the best I could… And although I fought it tooth and nail – since I became ill - she's had to completely take care of me.

• • • • •

My mom has always been a unique soul, she's often called a "little angel" by the people she encounters. You might think the adage: *If you don't have something nice to say, don't say it*, is a nice thing to teach your kids. But my mom lives according to the positive version of that rule, the one nobody ever bothers to tell their children: *If you have something nice to say, say it.*

And she does.

She tells strangers she likes their clothes or jewelry whenever she feels compelled. She'll compliment a stranger's smile then treat them to a meal just because they happen to be standing behind her in line. She can run into a couple walking their dogs down the street one minute, and the next minute they're over at our house for dinner. But she speaks nothing of karma – I'm not sure if I've ever even heard her use the word.

Our home growing up was always open to anyone who needed a place to be. While I was in high school she invited an alcoholic friend of my brother's and mine to live with her and I because she believed she could help him rebuild his life. A couple years later, she opened up our home to neighbors who were being evicted. A mother, father, their two-year-old and four-year-old daughters, and their dog moved into our house. She offered them three months rent-free, hoping that would be enough time for them to deal with their issues and get back on their feet.

The problem was, when she needed to kick out our friend who ended up drinking all the alcohol in the house and smashing the bottles in the backyard; when she needed to tell the family of four that their three months were up and they had to leave, or even when she decided she actually hated the couple she met walking the dogs and didn't even want them to stay for dessert... she turned to me.

Everyone knew they could depend on my mom. In turn I always made sure she could depend on me. By around the time my father left our roles – emotionally and otherwise - became very much reversed.

My mom was like my little girl. If her boss was rude to her, they'd have to answer to me. If she had a problem or needed advice, she'd come to me day and night. At times she'd ask not only for my opinion, but my permission to do or say things, which I'd have to remind her wasn't my place. There have been a handful of times where she'd slip and call me mom. And for a long time, that's how I felt.

Anyone who becomes ill must face the challenge of learning how to give up control, learning how to become reliant all over again. In my case, this transition was not only beyond frustrating but nearly extinct territory to try to recall upon.

The sicker I became the more I needed help with even the simplest tasks like getting my own food. I would call my mom crying in the morning on the phone in the other room to ask for some bread because I was throwing up bile and needed something to soak up the acid. It would take me at least an hour every morning to get over my ego before I made that call. I fought it with every fiber of my being. I don't know what I hated more, needing help, or needing help from someone who had given my brother and I everything and deserved nothing more than a *break*.

Before I was sick I had loved treating my mom to the things she refused to treat herself to. I used to save my money and surprise her. I once saved up enough to take her on a surprise week-long spa trip in Costa Rica. We explored rain forests and volcanoes, surfed in Jaco, rented Vespas, jumped off boats. I found out later however that all those years she had told me she dreamed of going to Costa Rica, she had really meant to say Cabo San Lucas. She'd just gotten the name wrong.

She cracks me up.

I always thought when I would come back home it would be to help her fix up and sell the house because I would have hit the jackpot - gotten a record deal, and finally have enough money to buy her the horse ranch that she'd always dreamed of. I never expected to be back there because I couldn't do anything without her help.

I never expected to bring back with me a colossal debt instead of an enormous fortune, and I hated myself for it.

Being a burden is like a thickness that lives in the air, it fills the entire house. It seeps through the vents. Every time I breathe I can taste it.

20 how to calculate the speed of screwed

Have you ever gone twenty-four hours without sleeping?
How about forty-eight?
How about seventy-two?

Most nights after Dad died, I couldn't sleep more than a half an hour at a time – but I also couldn't get out of bed. I was prescribed pills for the nausea, a side effect from the medications I was on, but it didn't make a dent.. Nothing got rid of the taste in my mouth – the stench of alcohol that seeped up through my esophagus –that smell of my insides, fermenting.

I was given pharmaceutical grade sleep aides for the insomnia, first Ambien, it didn't work. Next we tried Lunesta, nothing again. I tried a higher dose of each, no sleep, no luck. I was prescribed Trazadone, an even stronger medication, I took it and was up for the next forty eight hours. Little to no sleep on such a nightly basis was becoming dangerous, my nervous system was already a wreck; like a telephone wire accidentally snapped by a man trying to steal free cable – my nerves smacked against the ground in a panic– sparks flew.

My extreme sleep deprivation left me with a distorted and painful consciousness. I could no longer read or write. I watched all 222 episodes of *Roseanne* and all 293 episodes of *Beverly Hills 90210* a countless number of times. I then became overwhelmed with the urge to watch my old VHS copy of *Field of Dreams*. I watched it at least twice a day for three months straight… approximately 270 times.

The days blended. I never knew whether it was morning or night.

I found little relief from my symptoms. I had no intentions of continuing to live if I had to live without progress. I despised being a burden and acknowledging what I had become filled me with rage. I lay in my bed alone as my legs threw tantrums, kicking giant holes through my wall with my feet.

I took extra painkillers and turned on *Field of Dreams*, it was 4:00 a.m. Finally, I blacked out. I opened my eyes and looked at the clock: 4:29 a.m.

"FUCK!" I screamed, realizing sleep had eluded me again.

I lifted my fist and shattered the glass out of my window. Everyone around me knew I wasn't going to last much longer.

The doctors pulled out the big guns, GHB.

GHB is the "date rape" drug. It is known in the pharmaceutical world as Xyrum, a highly potent form of GHB, which is very rarely prescribed. A doctor specializing in sleep hooked me up to electrodes and kept me over night in a clinic. He prescribed me Xyrum after reading from the forty-five minutes of sleep he could record.

GHB will apparently knock you out, send you into such a deep sleep that you may not remember it at all. I was told that it would finally do the trick.

On this drug your muscles relax to the point that some patients actually experience urinating and defecating during their sleep.

Attractive, eh?

I had to follow *very* specific instructions: Do not eat or drink anything after six p.m., Measure every drop of the medicine *extremely* carefully to not accidentally overdose, Get into bed immediately after taking the medicine because there is no way you can move once it hits you. And last but not least, wear a diaper.

I came out of the bathroom holding onto the walls for support. A huge adult diaper stuck out from underneath my long johns.

"I'm bringing sexy back," I told my mom wryly who was standing outside waiting for me. She had agreed to sleep on a little futon we moved next to my bed to make sure I had no allergic reaction to my first dose. She had promised to stay awake – watch TV – for at least an hour to make sure I was okay.

I climbed into bed and drank the concoction. I readjusted my diaper under my blankets. It was one of those moments where you can't help wondering how on earth this could *possibly* be your life.

"Mom? You're awake right?" I asked feeling a numbness slowly begin to swallow my legs.

"Mom?!"

"Yeah, yeah… what?" She said startled, then remembered to quickly assure me, "I'm awake, I'm awake."

Within a half hour my whole body went numb. I couldn't move my arms or legs. My face felt as if it had disappeared – melted into my pillow and ran into the sheets.

"Mom?"
Silence.

'Okay, I'm okay.' I thought to myself, 'I'm just going to fall asleep any second now. I will sleep just like I did when I was a baby, just like the doctor said and I won't notice all these side effects, I'll be asleep in 3… 2…

Hmm… still here. '

'Okay,' I assured myself, 'it's going to kick in and knock me out right….
NOW!'

Fuck.

"M-m?"

Oh shit. I couldn't form words anymore. I couldn't feel anything and I couldn't form words and I couldn't fall asleep – it wasn't working. 'What if I stop breathing?' I started to panic.

I tried to turn myself over – I couldn't. I opened my eyes. Everything had blended together. My room had been replaced with thick wet paint. Everything smeared.

Three hours went by. I could tell by the sounds coming from the TV, I had memorized the Nick at Nite lineup long ago.

I tried swallowing. My throat was dry – making me overly conscious of my breathing. If I couldn't feel anything then maybe my body was shutting down – maybe my lungs would give up and I wouldn't even know.

"M—mm?"
I couldn't *believe* she fell asleep on me!
'Is this what a coma feels like?'
"M—mm?"

I finally was able to move my fingers slightly… I practiced over and over again until I could finally snap. I snapped again and again until she woke up.

"I wasn't asleep!" My mom said as soon as she became conscious of the snap.

"w—t—r"
I am the tin man. This is what I have become.
"w—a—t---rrr"
"Water?" My mom asked.
I couldn't nod. I was trapped. I blinked. She poured.
I never fell asleep. After six long hours of completely conscious paralysis I slowly got back my ability to move.

At least I didn't shit my pants.

My home nurse and Dr. Harris were urgently alerted about my severe insomnia. He called the hospital and ordered my second PICC line. I went in for the surgery the next day. We began the IV antibiotics full force that night.

I slept like a baby.

• • • • •

My IV and oral antibiotic treatment was steady. Fall passed - though living in my bedroom it was hard to tell. Days continued to blur into weeks, weeks blurred into months.

I can't remember much but medicine. Every once in a while I had a small distraction, a random companion, a conjugal visit.

I know I made out with a guy I'd gone to high school with but he kissed like a girl which kind of defeated the point. I know I slept with an eighteen-year-old Marine. She had contacted me about my music and ended up in my bed. One night my mom called a massage therapist to come help me and in the most conspicuous "whoops I left something behind" flirtatious move I have ever witnessed, she actually left her massage table in my room. Seriously, the table! She came over the next night "off-duty" and continued to "accidentally" leave the table three more times. Most of these people were as dumb as stones but quite easy on the eyes. Plus, it isn't easy getting any when you're bedridden.

New Years passed and my PICC line broke. Dr. Harris took no chances this time. I was back in the hospital the next day for PICC number three.

Harris wasn't impressed with how slow my body was fighting. He decided it was time to kick it up a notch. He convinced me, although exhausted and worn, that if I could give it all I had over the next six months, if I could just hang on a little longer, we would finally see the turn around we had been waiting for. After two and a half years of this disease tormenting me, I honestly didn't know how much more I could give, how much longer I could fight.

The new game plan included a change a venue. We were bringing hyperbaric oxygen treatment (HBOT) into my regime; One and a half to two hours a day, five days a week. We decided to continue the Avelox IV drip I had been on for three months and double the Rocephin IV infusions to twice a day instead of once, making a total of three IVs a day. On top of this I would continue the medication to keep my gallbladder from crystallizing, as well as a mixture of other heavy antibiotics and antivirals. We would add to that a large dose of malaria medication, plus a group of homeopathic drops and pills to build up my immunity and help kill off the co-infections. With my pain medication this amounted, as I said at the start, to ninety-seven pills and drops a day.

My scuba diving cousin hooked me up with Dr. Potkin who runs two HBOT centers in Los Angeles. Starting February, I would move into my aunt and uncle's home in Santa Monica.

My mom couldn't manage all the medical bills, loans, and constant fights with collectors and insurance companies. I overheard her talking about losing our house. I hadn't been able to read more than an email since my second to last semester of college; I was no help at all.

To say my mom and I were screwed was an under-statement. As Roseanne would put it, we were so far beyond screwed the light from screwed would take one billion years to reach earth.

After a million hoops I was finally found disabled by the federal government who gave me a whopping six hundred dollars a month to live off of. I gave everything I could to my mom. It didn't even cover a week of the medications I was on.

I was given an adult advocate by an organization, a woman named Julie who would help speak to these collectors on our behalf. On our fourth meeting, after I had already given her my bank account numbers, my social security number, my health insurance codes... she decided it was time to share with me her political and religious beliefs. She rubbed her silver Jesus fish that hung around her neck between her fingers as she told me how strongly she felt about banning gay marriage. I told her she was talking about people like me, my chance to maybe get married someday in this country. She informed me that homosexuality was nothing more than possession of one's body by the devil.

I pushed all my hair to one side and attempted my best Donald Trump impression. I then kindly asked her to get the fuck out of my house.

My mom and I were up the creek again.

21 anybody want a lime green margarita?

"If any of you could not afford to make a monetary donation tonight, I am also accepting sexual favors." I said soberly as I looked out at the crowd.

"That includes you miss Erin Foley." I joked and pointed to the famous young lesbian comic who was sitting in the corner. I could only make out the first few rows of people from under the spotlight. I thanked everyone for their help, explained that I truly did not know where I would be without it.

Private insurance and public medi-cal had refused to pay for a great deal of my treatment. It was costing us eight thousand dollars for HBOT. The insurance companies agreed that there has been a great deal of proof that these treatments work, that they are saving lives, but they were still considered experimental. I had no choice but to do them, I had no way to pay for them. I had to ask for help.

· · · · ·

I had gotten out of the car on Sunset Boulevard, outside the infamous black and white comedy store logo, across the street from the House of Blues. I walked passed the large line of people waiting at the door – stretched down the block. I

189

walked passed the bouncer and onto the red carpet. I had my purse hung over my shoulder and my IV drip stand in my hand, using it as a cane. A photographer stopped me and pushed me up next to Andy Dick - with his alcohol monitoring ankle bracelet - who had flown in from a gig in Florida to do the show. We hugged and the flashes went off. Surprisingly he made it through the entire night without getting arrested or putting his genitals on someone's face (as far as I know.) We posed in front of the press board that was donated from the TV show *Monk* and had The Comedy Store logo and the words Lyme-aid written in neon green across it a thousand times.

My brother had created an amazing benefit to raise money for my treatment. The whole event was surreal.

In a bizarre daze, I slowly walked up the stairs and passed two giant blown up photos of myself that my brother snatched from an interview I'd done for a magazine. I introduced myself to the incomparable Mo Collins (*Arrested Development, Parks and Recreation*) talked with the hilarious Jeff Ross (*Comedy Central*). My brother had just done a show with Jeff for his DVD in a sold out three-tiered venue in Atlantic City.

I walked into the lobby to find people being served free lime green margaritas. The drinks were being handed out by scantly dressed models from a tequila company who donated their alcohol in exchange for the free advertisement. I looked around at the auction tables – clothes and shoes from skateboard companies, apparel from Kat Von D.'s

High Voltage Tattoo shop, gift certificates for restaurants, jewelry, and haircuts were being bid on by guests.

My brother had my music play in between sets, my voice blasting through the speakers of the main room. We were filled to capacity with people who knew of me, a few who knew me. My mom was surrounded by friends and family who were being incredibly supportive.

Considering I hadn't been out in public for a *very* long time, nor had seen almost *anyone* at all in what could have been years, I was – you could say – a little overwhelmed to say the least. I shook hands and smiled and gave hugs. It didn't make sense… being the center of attention for something I had no control over, for being too broke to be able to do what was needed to save my own life.

I walked around with a conflicting sense of extraordinary gratitude and extreme confusion. I grew up dreaming of nights on Sunset Boulevard, big venues packed with fans, cameras flashing, the greenroom full of talent, the mirrors surrounded by bright bulbs. You just don't expect it to happen because you're losing the battle of your life. You never expect the attention to show up, not for your talent, but for your biggest mistakes.

I ran into Luenell (*Borat*), the comic and actress, through the crowd and said hello. We bonded immediately – comparing my gold sparkle cowboy boots to her gold glittered jackets and skintight spandex pants. By the end of the night she deemed me family…

Never underestimate the bond of gold glitter.

I sat down amidst the crowd, wondering how in the world the word had spread to Bobby Brown who was now sitting a couple tables away. When I thanked him for coming he said, "yo, yo, no doubt, for real girl, check it." I guess that's his prerogative… Hey-o!

I set up my IV at the booth. I had a schedule to keep. I sat back laughing at some of the best comics in the business while the medicine ran through me. My brother in his slick black tuxedo emceed the show as one comic after another kept the crowd in an uproar; John Caparulo (*Chelsea Lately*), T.J. Miller (*My Idiot Brother*), *Saturday Night Live's* Dean Edwards who flew in all the way from New York City, Ian Edwards (*Comedy Central*), Laura Kightlinger (*Saturday Night Live*), Erin Foley (*Last Comic Standing*), Luenelle, Jeff, Andy, and Mo.

People were giddy, pulling out there cell phone cameras to record. Every comic there that night was a headliner, they had never done a show together before. Even more unique, each of them stayed to watch the others' sets which almost never happens in the stand-up world. Every comic not only donated their time but insisted on donating money as well. Every one of them was kind to me and generous, happy to do whatever they could.

We charged twenty bucks a head to come to the show which was a steal considering the line-up. The Comedy Store took nothing off the top, graciously providing the entire night at the venue as well as their crew for free.

It was all pretty unbelievable.

My mom and I went back to my aunt and uncle's house and sat on my bed. We began counting the money with our fingers crossed, grateful, hopeful. Along with the money from the show and the money raised from the auction of all the donated goods, we began sorting through the huge pile of envelopes the Comedy Store had created and left on every table for extra donations. They were filled with cash and little notes of hearts, smiley faces, and sweet well wishes. In one envelope I found a thousand dollar check from a woman I had never even met until that night.

It was mind blowing.

I reached for the last envelope in the pile. I opened it surprised to find it was a letter from my cousin, Abraham.

Abe is not only my cousin, but one of my closest friends. Only a year older than me, we attended McGill University together, lived practically in the same house for two years. He is one of the sharpest and most loyal people I know. He wasn't, however, one for sharing his feelings, so when I began reading the letter, I couldn't help but get choked up.

He wrote about how much my illness had affected him and how he was and had always been there for me, things I knew without him ever having to say. As I went to put back the letter into the envelope to save, I noticed a check. I shook my head and passed it over to my mom to see.

There was a check for twenty five hundred dollars.

I'll never be able to thank him and all the people who

showed up that night enough, I know I would not be here to tell this story without them. I will never be able to thank my brother enough for pulling it off.

We raised nine thousand dollars that night, enough to cover forty sessions of hyperbaric oxygen treatment and two months of intravenous antibiotics with my weekly nursing care. It was a great weight off my mother's back and mine. It gave us breathing room. It gave me a chance to focus solely on my treatment again. And for just a moment, it reminded me to not forget to have a little faith in humanity.

ʚ

22 we both hang on for dear life

I have spent all of spring in Los Angeles under my new even more relentless daily regimen. As of now, I've been in HBOT for three months.

HBOT feels kind of like laying in a spaceship to nowhere. There is no room in the narrow glass tube to sit up or really turn around. I'm not claustrophobic, so once I got used to the pressure in my ears, I handled treatment well. By the end of my first week I was at a depth and pressure level equivalent to being forty feet underwater.

HBOT fights Lyme on three fronts: For one, Lyme hides, but the pressure from the oxygen pushes the medication deeper through the body, into the extremities, into cells it may not have been able to reach. Secondly, there is a strain of Lyme cannot survive in oxygen saturation. Thirdly, the oxygen helps build up white blood cells which is a great asset for immunity and strength to continue fighting. The combination of the three can have a huge impact on recovery.

Jay, the tech nurse, is a very handsome black man in his early thirties with great eyelashes. He immediately took me under his wing. After some warmly tested waters, we began having in-depth conversations about politics and music. We are interested in many of the same writers and public intellectuals. Sometimes I stay late after my treatment to hang out with him. Some days I go with him down to the basement to close out the oxygen tanks as they shoot out great billows of steam across the room. We put on giant headphones that block out the noise and thick leather gloves to keep out the freezing temperatures. Some days I give him a ride and we smoke cigars and listen to Nina Simone.

Being in that tube has become normal to me. I guess anything can become normal when you do it long enough. I can stay calm, zone out on my favorite ridiculous storylines I have seen a thousand times before.

I only panicked once in the chamber. I had a high fever that afternoon, was having a rough day. I was locked into the chamber and the theme song to *90210* started up right on cue. Without thinking I began to whistle along.

The more I realized no noise was coming out of my mouth due to the immense depth and oxygen pressure, the more I became aware of where I was, the more I began to panic. I knew if anything happened there'd be no way for me to get out immediately. What if I began getting chest pains again, or had a seizure? I started thinking about an old woman I saw in one of the chambers my first week there, she began vomiting in the tiny cramped spaceship, crying and yelling while Jay tried to help. What if I needed to throw up – the pressure on my ears would be unbearable. It takes nearly fifteen minutes to bring you back up to level. Going any faster can bring serious consequences like the bends.

Jay noticed and picked up the phone. He talked me

through it, he calmed me down..

In case you ever find yourself in a Hyperbaric Chamber, I would highly recommend:

Do not try to whistle.

Dr. Harris has finally hit the right combination of drugs. Now I'm able to drive again so I spend the route to HBOT treatment every day the same way. On the way there, I turn up the Two Gallants *What the Toll Tells* album or Modest Mouse's old album *Lonesome Crowded West* with "Cowboy Dan." I play my stereo as loud as possible. I imagine Isaac from Modest Mouse and Gallants Adam and Tyson sitting there in the car with me; Adam in the back seat with his guitar and harmonica in hand next to Isaac, Tyson in the front seat next to me, smacking the copper snare from my drum set with a pair of sticks.

All the windows of my Oldsmobile are open. I imagine we have cigarettes hanging out of the sides of our mouths, dirt caked on our hands and trapped under our nails. I imagine we are barefoot, screaming their songs at the top of our lungs. I imagine we drive right past the HBOT center and get back onto the highway and out of Los Angeles; speeding through the side roads of the dry California desert till my old black car is covered in sand from the wind. Sometimes I imagine we pull up to a train station and Tyson opens the glove compartment to grab the black nickel Walther and sticks it into the waist of his jeans, behind his back. We rob a few couples then jump back into the car I've kept still running, and take off to the nearest saloon where we drink beer and dark whiskey and laugh as we play cards with our feet up on the table.

But everyday I pull up to South Beverly Drive instead and the boys disappear as I enter the darkness of the sterile cement parking garage under the medical building.

Everyday I drive back to my Aunt Tina and Uncle Arnie's house after treatment in silence as I face the sun on its way down over the pacific. I hit the same cross section of Santa Monica and Barrington and never cease to wonder where I am. The way the road heads up the small hill, the lettering – faded and chipped – on the otherwise bare building on the right corner of the street. I think for a moment I am on Cote-St.-Luc road at the corner of Saint Jacque back in Montreal, I believe for a moment it is 2003 and I am heading home, that I am going to see my dad. And I think for a moment that I could start again.

I know a decent amount of people in Los Angeles, but I haven't seen any of them. None of my friends from high school or college that live up here have bothered to come by. Nobody's brought by a movie or board game. Nobody's sent a mixed CD or a Mad libs. None of my friends went to Lyme-Aid to help ensure my treatment and survival. One did send a check.

I thought I knew a decent number of people in the world in general, but I'm beginning to realize they have all but disappeared.

I can see a little progress but treatment has gnawed at me slowly. Each day is another battle, most days harder than the one before. There is only one goal: fight each day best I can to ensure I may see another one.

Quantity seems to be the focus, quality is a concept fallen by the wayside.

I wake up, take my meds, do my IVs, go to treatment, take a nap, take my meds, do my IVs, go to sleep.

The nights are the hardest.
On a scale from one to ten, I'd say they are hell.

It is hell being in this bed every night with tubes sticking out of me, g-d knows what concoction of poisons making their way through my veins. Fighting a war between me and these monsters, each of us fighting for life, very much aware that both of us cannot survive.

It is purgatory to lie here night after night, reclaiming territory I was always misled to believe was mine.

And it is torture to lay here alone. It is a loneliness that I do not believe you can ever truly come back from. This is a loneliness that kills you slowly. This is a loneliness that changes you for good.

My room at my aunt and uncle's house is the playroom for their grandkids. It is a bed in the midst of piles of dolls with realistic looking eyes, plastic castles, mountains of crayons, and toy houses. It is like living on a green screen, a nonsensical set. I hung up a black sheet over the window to block out the sun. I turn on the fan I brought up, and turn off the one light in the room. I sit each day and night in the pitch black, in the middle of the bed in usually a white wife-beater and a pair of long johns, with my portable DVD player – the only thing I can see or hear in the darkness.

I live in a cave that I can only hope will turn out to be a tunnel. And as I imagine myself walking through it, my face cold and numb, my uniform ripped and worn, I believe I hold the hand of a little girl who drags her *90210* sleeping bag along the dirt-packed floor while she stares at her seven-inch screen. I try to stop and sit down in the dark with her – try to let her rest awhile as I vigilantly keep guard; her face lit up in a soft blue light. If I can get her out of here, at least I'll know I've done my all.

I am soothed for a moment by the familiar riff of a sweet harmonica, the laugh of an unflinching woman and the voice of a kind heavy man. In that darkness we lose ourselves in the belief of a simpler town, a place more loyal and honest… the belief in a happier life. She closes her eyes and I pray we'll wake up on the porch outside the Conner's house… on the corner of 3rd Avenue at 714 Delaware Street.

I am very much aware that my closet friends and family are fictional, but they sure as hell are consistent.

23 uh oh

My arm became infected last week. I remember a time when people were naïve enough to call me lucky.

"Squeeze my hand," my mom demanded but shouldn't have. She clenched her teeth while I dug my nails into her palm, feeling the bones in her fingers press against each other.

"I'm hurting you," I said.

"I don't care. Just don't touch your arm," she insisted. "When it hurts you, when you want to scratch it, just grab my hand and squeeze as hard as you need."

I didn't want to scratch my arm, I wanted to tear the whole fucking thing off. The clear bandage that covered my PICC line barely contained the infection trying to seep out. My skin was bleeding, peeling off underneath the airtight dressing. I wanted to grab the plastic tubes that hung off of my disintegrating flesh and pull. I wanted to feel it run through my body as I yanked it free. Forty centimeters of plastic that ran through my veins – exiting at the mess that had become my arm. Every nerve in my body was screaming, get this fucking line out!

I almost broke my mom's hand as we slowly walked around the mall on Pico, waiting for my appointment at the Hyperbaric treatment center nearby. My mom always said she would take my pain away from me if she could, this was the extent of how much of my pain I would ever let her feel.

"It hurts! It hurts!" I kept laughing... laughing like I always did when I was in pain, like a fool. It's always a little confusing for my doctors when I laugh until they get to know me. I laugh when I'm nervous. I laugh when the pain is too great to bear.

I sat shaking in the patient room. Dr. Potkin unwrapped the dressing from my arm. Those past excruciating hours were finally over – I could finally take a deep breath as he wiped alcohol across my anxious skin. The blisters were intense; the skin was infected. We did not know if the PICC line, and subsequently my heart, was infected as well... a risk we were all vigilantly trying to prevent from the start.

I held my breath again as I felt the line being gently pulled through my body, slipped out slowly through the hole in my arm - surreal release. I could feel the plastic lightly sweeping across the nerves. I let out my breath. The doctor tested the line and sent in a blood culture to check my heart for infection. He treated my arm and gave me a prescription to heal it.

The test results came back negative for my heart being infected, I don't know what I would have done if I had to deal with that on top of everything.

Within a half hour I had an appointment set up back in

San Diego to have another PICC line put in; It would be my fourth.

I was too tired from the infection and treatment to drive. My mom had gone back to San Diego for work before me so I decided to take the train.

My brother and I hit bumper-to-bumper traffic and I missed the first train I planned to take. We tried again a few hours later, there was an accident on the highway, I missed the second train. I finally got to the open halls of Union Station in downtown Los Angeles, in time to make their last train out. I wouldn't arrive till after midnight and I had to be at the hospital for outpatient surgery early the next morning.

This was a bad idea.

My dad Harry used to tell me that if you really want something you can always find a way to get it if you're clever enough. When the front door is locked, try the back, if the back door is bolted, climb through the window. I lived by that advice one hundred percent.

The trick is to decipher between what is a roadblock set up to test how hard you're willing to persist and what is a sign from the universe telling you to STOP.

Walls are not always dares tempting you to jump them, sometimes they are just signs to turn around.

I should have turned around.

My mom and I sat with the nurse in the waiting room while he went over the procedure with me. I had done this three times before, I had specific questions and demands. I was told by my doctor to make sure they inserted the PICC line into a different vein, so as not to overuse the one I had a line in for six months straight. I told them to make sure they used a Power Groshong, a kind of PICC line that has a valve inside which stops blood from flowing back into the line. It is much easier to use and safer. He assured me he would tell the radiologist who was performing the procedure.

I lay on the table, covered in sanitary sheets again, wide awake. They took my right arm and laid it out straight. The giant light of the movable ultrasound lit up my face and hurt my eyes. The light blurred the faces of the nurses and the doctor that stood over me – chatting with one another – preparing to start in a nonchalant manner. After they stuck the long needle into my arm to freeze it, they began.

All I could think about was the smell of bleach. And that Coldplay was playing quietly over the speakers in the operating room. I closed my eyes. I heard my pulse, steady on the monitor.

Beep….   Beep….   Beep…   Beep….

I thought about how I was going to get through this just like before and keep going just like before, when the music was cut suddenly by the sound of the surgeon's voice:

"Uh oh."

Uh oh? If Letterman made a top 10 list of things you do not want to hear during surgery, "uh oh" would be ranked at least at number 2, right under "has anybody seen my scissors?"

I must have imagined it.

"Uh oh."

He said it again. Are you fucking kidding me? This was not in my head. Neither was the screaming that followed.

"WE NEED HELP OVER HERE! WE NEED HELP OVER HERE NOW! I NEED A NURSE NOW! "

Oh my g-d. What's happening? I saw nurses come running in from the next room.

"DON'T MOVE! DON'T MOVE!"

They yelled at me while they lifted me on the table high. They scattered their faceless bodies around me, rearranging my limbs, grabbing things I couldn't see.

I did not move.

Fucking shit. I am going to die in a messy operating room full of tubes hanging all over the walls. I am going to die under big bright lights. That smell. The bleach. I am going to die in a room that smells of bleach while listening to people scream over Coldplay. I cannot die to fucking Coldplay!

My dear mother was right outside in the waiting room. I thought about her sitting there quietly unknowing that her daughter could die down the hall while she was thumbing through a Reader's Digest.

I could hear my heart on the monitor getting faster, cutting through the thoughts running through my head:

BEEP! BEEP! BEEP-BEEP-BEEP-BEEP!

Some people, like my mom have had out-of-body experiences when they're so close to dying. But this was different, I could smell the breath of death on my face. I could feel my soul trying like hell to hold on tightly to my body, gripping with white knuckles to not be grasped away. I knew if I let go I would never bother coming back. My chest tightened.

I felt the blood rushing away from my face.
I felt the blood flowing over my arm – wet – warm.
I felt my breath clench – my lungs tight.

"GRAB THE CLAMP! GRAB THE FUCKING CLAMP!"

The doctors scrambled.
I felt the tightness release. I heard my heartbeat returned to near normal. I looked to my right and saw the piles of rags covered in blood.

Minutes later they wrapped up my arm and helped me sit up.

"What happened?" I asked. The radiologist who performed the surgery had split. The nurse pretended she didn't know.

"You lost a lot of blood" was all she said. I was too dizzy to get up. Where was the nurse to go over the PICC line instructions with me? Where was the nurse to make sure I knew what to do next? They said nothing. They gave me nothing, no handout, no paperwork.

I got myself up and walked through the double doors alone and saw my mother's expression when she saw that all color was gone from my already pale face. I saw her eyes and I doubled over into tears. She brought me over to a chair in the middle of the great room in the hospital where I fell into the seat and hung my head. I sobbed – out of confusion, out of relief, out of the fear that had no chance in that room to escape.

My arm was cold, my hand and forearm completely numb. This had never happened before. I couldn't stop shaking. My mom got the nurse. It was a nurse who enjoyed speaking in funny accents, no joke. He told me, "well, maybay, blimey, they used too much freezing!" He thought that was why my arm and hand were ice cold and numb, which didn't end up going away for another twenty-four hours. He was useless. And he was wrong.

They had severed my artery.
I could have died.

I got home from the surgery feeling like a ghost. I looked at the line. It was in the wrong vein, the one that had been overused. It was also the wrong PICC line; it had two separate valves for absolutely no reason whatsoever. It was not a Power Groshong so blood could come in and out of the tubes as it pleased which meant I had to constantly use Heparin on both valves or else I risked getting a blood clot. I was exhausted. I turned on the TV.

As I sat on my bed, trying not to concentrate on the pain throbbing in my arm, the multi-pronged mistake sticking out, trying to regain my nerves from the procedure itself, I felt my leg was suddenly wet.

I looked down.

A puddle of blood was forming on my right thigh. Confused as hell I pulled down my long johns to see if I was cut. I wasn't, the blood wasn't coming from my leg.

I checked my arm and saw the blood was coming from the line. Dripping slowly, steadily... The PICC line was *open*.

They were in such a rush to get me out of the hospital that they did not even check to make sure they closed the cap on the end of the line properly. The only thing that had been keeping my blood from coming out of the line was a tiny clamp – smaller than my pinky fingernail. It had accidentally been clicked open – easily - without notice when I sat down on my bed. If I hadn't seen the blood on my leg, if I would have fallen asleep like I did after almost every procedure, then I would have bled out to death in my sleep.

I would have been found in the morning in my bed, my clean white sheets, soaked in all the blood my heart could have pumped out – a heart that thought it was doing nothing more than its job to make me live.

Quietly, through an accidentally left open cap by the rushed hands of embarrassed hospital workers, all my blood would have been drained from my body, all my blood would have been gone.

I would have never felt a thing.

24 a life to no longer get back to

My Aunt and Uncle are back in town. I saw them this morning before treatment. My Aunt asked me the same question I have heard a million times since the day I was diagnosed. They have been incredibly generous, letting me live in there guest room for nearly six months now. But that question, even if meant with whole-hearted kindness, still rubbed me the wrong way:

Are you excited to get your life back?

Anyone who has suffered from a critical illness has probably heard those words one time or another, sometimes spoken with genuine naivety, sometimes with an obnoxious new-aged patchouli pungent undertone, but let's start with this:

Please recognize that question is as loaded as a fat baby's diaper.

There is no life to get back to. That life is *gone*.

The first phone call I had with Maria after I was bit in Virginia, I was warned of the world on the horizon. "Get ready," she said, "because you are going to have your entire world turned upside down. If you get out of it at least 95% of your friends will be gone."

"There are people in your life for the wrong reasons," she continued.

I thought she was exaggerating. I thought I could wrap my head around it but I had no idea what I was really in for. Illness forces you to test friendships in a way nobody should ever have to. It weeds out the strong from the weak, the loyal from the superficial, it begs the question, when I lose everything, when I need you most, will you be there?

In my case, that question was returned with a resounding, choir-like:

NOOOOOOOOOOOOO.

You can go back and dissect yourself, your friendships, until the end of time. You can wonder what you did wrong, why you never noticed the little things before, the imbalances, how you could have somehow warned yourself that these people would not be there when the chips were down. You can spend nights on end not sleeping, just wondering, 'did they even ever love me in the first place?'

'Cause I tell you this, if they didn't, they should all win Emmys, and not daytime ones at that.

I was the kind of person who took my friendships very seriously, took deep pride in them. Most of the friendships I had were at least ten years old, through transitions of adolescence into young adulthood. These people were more than friends to me, they were family. The truth is you simply do not know how people will react when you need them until you do. You can't ask them what they would do... everybody wants to believe the best in themselves.

All the social friends I had in New York City, the ones I had known for years and spent many of drunken nights singing Karaoke with in Hell's Kitchen, going with to parties, chatting endlessly about everything… were gone before I filled up my tank and hit the George Washington Bridge. I never received a single email or call from any of them again.

My longtime childhood friends were no better, the best friends I'd ever known, the ones I used to plan the future with. The ones I shared dreams with, like creating art together, buying houses near each other one day, imagining having children around the same time so that our kids could grow up together, fall in love and get married. The ones I once oft spoke to till sunrise. They dropped off one by one… each loss breaking me down a little more than the last.

When you start to come out of an illness you trick yourself into believing you will be greeted as if you are returning home from war. You hope that people have awaited your return. You imagine receiving a medal for your bravery. You picture that long lost love in the back of your mind, grabbing you at your arrival, telling you of the devastation they would've felt if you'd never made it back to shore.

You believe *if* you survive, you will be met with more than a stack of unpaid bills, a hundred grand in debt, and threatening letters from collectors. You think, *if* you make it, you might come out the other side with more than a case of post-traumatic stress disorder and a dependency on pain medication. Maybe it's our generation, maybe it's this country, but people do not wait. Young people, especially, do not know how to be there for someone who is going through a great illness or loss.

An emoticon is not a hug. A posting on Facebook that says, "I hope you're feeling better!" is not equivalent to sharing a meal. These robotic and overused gestures are not equivalent to *time*!

I have heard that some of these people didn't know any better, but I say to hell with them. In the words of Dylan McKay I too shall proclaim:

May the bridges I burn light my way.

I went into treatment today and I lost it in front of Jay. That question: *Are you excited to get your life back?* kept playing over and over again in my head.

For nearly three years I had fallen into the trap of believing it was possible! But in that life that I've been trying to get back to, that life before I became sick, I had an amazing best friend, and I had an incredible and intimate friendship with a girl named Sara, I had a bandmate and childhood friend named Jen. In that life I had a phone that rang straight through the night. I have dreams of New York City, of my apartment with Mekia and Peter; But Mekia and Peter are married now, living on their own, their daughter is already two and they have another little girl on the way. That apartment? It's no longer mine. My classmates have turned their tassels from right to left and are now on their way to graduate from law schools and masters programs throughout the country. In that life I've been trying to get back to... I had a dad, now he's gone.

Even if I could get it all back, that life I had before was one where I did not know what it was like to have my own life dangle in the balance by the thin skin of teeth. This knowledge doesn't go away when you get well. This is a knowledge you do not come back from.

That life that everyone is telling me I'll get back to is nothing more than a mirage. There is no water there, just charred fragments left over from a world burned down.

That life is gone and it's never coming back again.

25 motherf*cker!

I have been incredibly sad since my realization… I've been trying to figure out how to mourn a life that everyone mistakenly thinks you're still living.

But a few days ago, the strangest thing happened. I closed my eyes and heard the loud pop behind me as Jay turned the heavy locks on the chamber door and the air rushed out. My ass was still sore from the intramuscular shot of Rocephin I had received right before going into the hyperbaric oxygen chamber.

They had to remove my fourth PICC line only a week after they had put it in. Apparently my veins had enough. The blisters returned and covered my right arm. It turns out I've developed allergies to not only the tape and supposed hypoallergenic bandages, but even the chloraprep used to clean the site itself which has left burns on my skin.

I am now being shot with a three-inch needle every day into my ass muscle instead.

… Good times.

There is no room to move around in the tube, no way to sit up. Most people lay perfectly still while inside, I did too, at the beginning. But 35 plus treatments in, nearly 70 hours inside, I can't take it anymore. I've started spending half my time in the chamber trying to turn myself upside down – I tuck my legs in tight against my chest and stick my bare feet against the two-foot ceiling. I roll around like a monkey.

The only other patient I ever saw acting like me was seven.

Earlier the other day during treatment, Jay accidentally hit the wrong remote and turned the channel in the middle of the last ten minutes of the *series* finale of *Beverly Hills 90210* which always made me cry. I had watched the entire series through the year and we were finally at the last episode. With tears running down my cheeks I started banging against the glass with my fist to get his attention.

"Quick!" I yelled laughing, "Change it back!! David and Donna are about to get *married*!"

The series finished, flipped over, and started the pilot again. My feet and hand-prints were all over the glass on the inside of the tube. I kept my eyes closed as Jay slid the gurney out. I had one hand holding onto my waist. I was wearing pants three times my own size. I had accidentally worn the wrong type of pajama pants that day and luckily Jay noticed. Anything other than 100% cotton can cause a spark and burst into flames in the chamber having set me, and subsequently the entire building, on fire in the explosion that would have followed.

I didn't want to wear a gown two years ago when I was in the hospital and I didn't want to wear one now. Jay gave me an extra pair of his 2XL light blue scrubs. I felt the wheels click into place; Jay was standing behind me holding onto the bars of the gurney. I opened my eyes to the surprising sight of a woman's face over me.

"What are you in here for?" She asked bluntly, before I even had the chance to sit up. Nobody ever asked each other that. I looked at her before I answered. I knew that face but couldn't place it. She was in her street clothes and all parts of her body that were showing were covered in gorgeous ornate tattoos that weaved themselves in and out of her bright black skin. Her thick dreads hung down a little past her neck. She waited for my answer.

"Lyme disease," I told her, smiling at her boldness and stretching as I pulled myself off the gurney and tied the strings of my pants tighter, hoping they didn't fall off. "I know you don't I?" I asked trying to put it together, "from TV, eh?"

"Maybe," she smirked. "I was in this little sketch comedy show called Mad TV. So what does Lyme disease do? Just make you tired or something right?"

Her face clicked with a thousand scenes in my head.

I put out my hand.

"I'm Debra," she said.

"I know."

I remembered her cracking me up from her unrivaled impressions of Oprah Winfrey, Whitney Houston... her characters flailed through my memory, I had seen her face a million times – she had always made me smile. This woman was a brilliant comic and actress.

"It's pretty complicated," I explained unsure if she was just being polite or really wanted to know. She waited for me to continue, so I did. I proceeded to give her a concise run down of the last three years... what had happened to my brain, my body, my life. In those few minutes I watched her face turn from humorous and friendly, to that of a woman who was highly invested and intensely concerned. She hadn't expected to get the answer I had given her. She figured I was there to help heal faster from surgery, like her.

Jay smiled at me. He had set this up.

Jay had scheduled me to be out of treatment at the same time as she was coming in. Debra had come in a couple days before and Jay had realized that her and I needed to meet. He didn't realize, however, how explosive and significant the meeting between us would be. She asked me more questions and I answered. I told her how many treatments I was in for, what my day to day life was like. Then I shut my mouth.

"What the fuck?! Are you serious?!" She asked me beginning to raise her voice. "Motherfucker! Do you realize what a blessing it is that you are still here goddess?"

I nodded quietly.

She shook her head back and forth, her smile had faded completely, she stared intently at me. "I can't believe this happened to you," she said. "Everyone you run into everyday is complaining about their lives, people are so desperate to get more, more, more… everyone is so desperate for such petty materialistic things, they do not understand what they have at all!" Jay had stopped working and fell silent as well.

"It is as if everyone is walking around this world with a cup in their hand, waiting for g-d to fill it with water. And people *squeeze* that cup so hard, they ignore what they have - they are so desperate for water that when water comes they have *squeezed that cup* so hard it has broken!! It can no longer hold any water at all!!" She squeezed her fist so tightly I could practically see the water rush over it.

"But you goddess!" she continued as she began to walk slowly across the room, forcefully, deliberately, like a preacher at a Sunday service. "You have been through hell and back. Do you know the number of ways you could have fallen off the precipice?! Or given up? Or JUMPED!? You were on that precipice and you are still alive to tell about it! You do not hold that cup in desperation. You will be *ready* when that cup is filled, and believe me *your cup will be filled goddess!*"

I was frozen.

I thought she might have accidentally walked into the wrong book.

All of a sudden I found someone who understood. She was affected. She did not feel sorry for me, she was proud of me, and her pride and empathy were too much to contain.

I don't know what you believe in, but I believe we have guardian angels on this earth, and I am pretty sure that day I met one of mine.

All the windows blew open and she filled the room with light. I hadn't realized how dark it was in there until I saw what happened when she spoke.

When she paused, Jay delicately interrupted, gave

her a gown and told her she needed to get changed for treatment. She went into the conjoined room and closed the door behind her. I sat down in a chair and looked over at Jay who looked back speechless.

"MOTHERFUCKER!"

Debra had started yelling again from behind the door. We both cracked a startled smile, not knowing what to say.

"Look at what G-d did for you goddess! He sent a psychic! He sent a weather girl! He got all these people together to pay for your treatment. He saw the road blocks and he found another way!"

She came out into the main room again. It was hard to comprehend - this strong driven voice was coming from a striking petite woman, now wearing nothing but a hospital gown. I could see all her beautiful tattoos now and as I stood back up she took my hands. "There is a prayer that is important to me and I want to say it to you," she said. She wrapped her arms around me before I could respond.

"G-d bless, be well, stay well," she recited softly to me. "Peace and prosperous abundance always for everything that you deserve in this life time. In this here. In this now.

"In the name of your Higher Power. In the name of your Higher Self. And in the name of your higher good towards others. Amen," she finished but waited a few seconds before letting me go.

"You are amazing." I said quietly, finally finding myself able to speak out loud again. I wiped away the tears that had fallen onto my face.

"Thank you goddess," she replied, "how sweet it is of you to see yourself in me."

"No, no, no," I said shaking my head and smiling, "I think you are unbelievable."

"Thank you goddess," she repeated, this time bringing her hands to my shoulders. She looked intently into my eyes and this time slower, she continued, "how sweet it is of you to see yourself in me."

She waited for my face to show I understood, that there would be no arguing, that I would have no choice but to accept this compliment.

We talked for over an hour, forcing Jay to stay far later than he had expected to, but he wasn't bothered. All I could say was thank you over and over again for all she had brought to me – Love. Hope. Kindness.

Debra asked Jay if he could reschedule her next treatment so that her and I could have treatment together.

"I do not bring people into my life lightly," she told me before leaving, "and you are family now, that is just how it is..."

• • • • •

Today I came into treatment to find Jay smiling. He pulled out a beautifully decorative envelope with my name on it and a small lace bag stitched with roses in red and gold.

"Guess who came by for you?" He asked as he handed the gifts to me.

I opened the envelope to find a card with a picture of a girl with a tattoo of a guitar painted across her back. I sat down next to Jay and read the letter:

Goddess,

Your light is brighter than you have yet to discover. The more you do, the more the Universe reveals. Your journey is riveting but not as much as the journey yet taken. The 'goddess necklace' represents the principals of power and protection: The angel is for protection. Her wings fold into a heart for love. The Ethiopian Koptic cross represents faith. The Buddha is for peace and surrender. His peaceful expression is peace and his eyes closed are for meditation and ultimately, surrender. May you be loved and protected. May you walk in faith. May you find peace and surrender to your journey, and receive every abundant blessing you deserve for all you've gone through. G-d bless, be well, stay well. Peace and abundance always.

Love,
Debra xoxo

I opened the lace bag and put on the necklace, it was intricately formed with small iridescent clear beads, the three silver symbols hung down in the middle and laid against my chest. My old life may have been gone, but there was a new life coming. I mourned the life I lost but Debra exposed me to the world after, a world post illness, a world beyond the wreckage and the flames.

My past was dead... and I'm beginning to realize something about that is beautiful.

26 july 5th, 2009

Today is July 5th, 2009.

I finally finished all my major treatment last week.

I moved back home with my mom in San Diego and waited to see what would show up on what had become the most ominous day of the year, yesterday... the Fourth of July.

Yesterday evening my mom and I hit the I-15 East through the tight roads over the mountains towards the casino where the concert was being held. I could see the thousands of people gathered outside ready to celebrate, lit up by the lights around the stage and the sun going down around the canyon.

Kristin, a family friend, is the wife of Robert DeLeo, the bassist of Stone Temple Pilots. Over the last three years she has asked me to come with her to see the band a few times but only last night did I finally have the opportunity to say yes.

Kristin and her parents met us at the gate with the tickets and laminated V.I.P. passes that we hung over our necks. We made our way through the bouncers and the busy crowd and past another set of guards towards the trailers.

I walked past the huge metal black bars that formed the structure of the stage, past a group of music engineers standing over the twenty foot long mixing board. I watched people in black carry equipment passed us, everyone scrambling, awaiting the night to begin. We walked to the row of trailers – dressing rooms for each of the band members – and entered the greenroom. As I walked in I realized I began doing something I hadn't done in years, I dreamed.

I looked at the leather couches, the choices of soymilk, juice, and sodas spread out across the table. I scanned the multicolored decorative silk sheets that had been hung up over the windows and on the walls per request by the band and I began fantasizing about the kinds of things I would have backstage before a show, what I would want on my rider someday. I imagined, like them, creating my own world before I'd go on stage.

I introduced myself to Eric Kretz and Dean Deleo, the drummer and guitarist of the band. I told them I had been listening to them since I was in fourth grade and they laughed as I accidently made them feel old. They were friendly and relaxed. Stone Temple Pilots had been one of the first bands I remember loving, they were one of the first bands who inspired me at a young age to play rock and roll.

Kristin introduced me to her husband Robert who I had not yet had the chance to meet. He gave me a huge hug and told me how happy he was that I was well enough to be there. He was incredibly kind and gracious, talking to me for quite a while about music and what I had been dealing with. He had to get changed to get ready for the show, I couldn't wait to see him play.

Kristin and I sat with her parents and my mom at an outdoor table next to the greenroom. I overheard the people at the next table talking about Scott Weiland, the singer and front man of the band.

Strangers blathered on about how Scott thought he was Jesus, how he thought he was too good to show up early or talk to people before the show.

That's how people used to talk about me. People always misread my loneliness and inability to connect with arrogance.

The people at the other table gossiped about how Scott had decided he wanted a break from the band at one point and lost the other band members millions of dollars in touring money. You can replace a band member, no matter how amazing and talented they are, but the welfare of the band, the livelihood of the crew and the families of the other band members – literally hundreds of people - were all on the shoulers of Scott to continue to play, to show up.

I asked Kristin if Scott was here yet.

"No," she explained, "he comes literally minutes before and leaves immediately after."

I was told by a number of people that evening that even if I did see Scott, it was pointless to try to say hi, he refuses to talk to anyone.

The show was about to begin, Kristin took my mom and I to the gated-off pit in front of the stage. It had been years since I had been to a concert, the air was electric as the lights went down and the canyon became black.

In a flash the music hit the audience like a wave, the lights hit finding Scott in the middle of the stage with a cowboy hat on and a long white suit. The whole band transformed – they were no longer the calm well-tempered kind men I had just spoken with but were now forces of nature.

I closed my eyes.

I didn't need to look to know how bright it was.

Kristin tapped my mom and I and told us to follow her. We passed the guards and began walking the slender black metal staircase up to the stage. With every step I felt a part of me begin to believe that someday I would walk those steps on my way to my own show, on my way to playing music again.

We walked onto the stage and over to the right side where Robert's bass guitars were lined up in a row, tuned and ready to be run out to him at any time. We stopped and I stood there, watching the rest of the show feet from the band, feet from the edge of the stage and the thousands of people screaming – all overpowered by the tremendous energy the music sent them as they threw it right back.

The power was palpable. It was awing, crushing.

And as I stood on that stage and listened to the music, I could remember the girl who had grown up playing their CDs, who still knew all the words, the girl who loved music in it's purest form, not as a source to get her somewhere better. I remembered the girl who had been inspired to create.

And I thought about where she had been on this night years before, and where she had gone.

When the show was over, we headed back to the tables outside the greenroom. It was full of family and friends of the band, everyone celebrating the incredible show, congratulating Robert and Eric and Dean, their children running around while the nannies kept watch. Out of the corner of my eye, I saw Scott sneaking past everyone and heading down the stairs to make a quick exit. The people around me whispered and the mood fell quiet.

"Hey Scott!" I yelled, putting down my water and getting up out of my chair.

Everyone at the surrounding tables looked at me. I walked down the stairs and over to the man everyone was talking about. This man, who along with the likes of Kurt Cobain, Trent Reznor, Maynard James Keenan… had made me want to be a singer and a writer as a child, had inspired me to throw myself into every vocal line and transform myself as soon as the music began.

He stopped walking.
"Sorry to yell,"
"It's no problem," he said gently smiling.

My heart broke when I looked into his eyes. He looked crushed under the person he had become, the person he was supposed to be. He had a loneliness within him that I had yet only seen within myself. I looked next to him to see a petite Hispanic woman with a uniform from the casino hotel holding a plate of food with a large metal cover on top. I realized he had no family there that night to greet him, no friends, no lover, no kids waiting backstage.

"I just wanted to tell you the show was beautiful, you were beautiful," I said.

"Thank you, that's very sweet of you," he smiled, asking my name.

I talked with him about the influence he had on me becoming an artist, and why I hadn't been able to come to a show with Kristin before.

"Jesus," he said, "I'm so sorry to hear that."

He spoke sincerely, quietly. He put his arms around me and gave me a long hug. He held me tightly. It was the saddest hug I've ever known.

I looked around at the people watching with confusion, some in disbelief. He told me the woman next to him had his dinner and was waiting to take him back to his room at the hotel. I wished him well and he hugged me again in the same heartbreaking way.

I saw this man who knew how to give through music, who could say what he wanted in his lyrics, who was sensuous and passionate and yet somehow, that night, still appeared disconnected, beaten-down, alone; Somehow still in a great deal of pain.

…So here's the thing, I can't tell you I 'm grateful this illness happened to me. And I can't tell you that it taught me to really value the fragility of life – because that's bullshit, I didn't need to almost lose my life to understand what I had sadly learned long before. I can't tell you this illness brought me some religious experience because if anything it grounded me to the earth. If anything it made me feel like we do not need to physically die to experience heaven or hell… that everyday we experience good and evil right here on earth.

But I will say this; when I looked at Scott I saw myself. And I know that if this illness had not happened, in some sense or another, he is who I would have become.

• • • • •

Things didn't change in an instant. The truth is, most of the time I forget that *everything* is different, except in moments:

When I raise my hands above my head in the shower without it being too exhausting and painful to wash my hair. When I walk down an aisle in the grocery store and realize I am not in a wheelchair or holding onto a walker or cane. When I eat cereal and realize the flakes actually made it to my mouth instead of falling off halfway because the tremors are so bad. When I hear myself using words once long lost. When I chase Junior in the backyard and see the patch of grass that was sat on for hours by a girl unable to speak.

I know things are different when I see the plaster covering the deep holes in my walls or the cardboard covering what was once a glass window and I remember this bedroom used to bear the brunt of rages. When I don't scream at the sound of a loudspeaker that goes off at a department store, when I sleep through the night, I can see it. I know things are different when I wake up in the morning and remember I do not have a tube laced up to my heart. When I wake up in the morning well... I know it is finally over.

This disease was fought to the death, but undeniably death did take place. I always thought one would *have* to survive: the person or the disease. But I was wrong. In the end, they killed each other. In the end it was mutual destruction. In the end, the girl fighting the monsters is as dead as the monsters themselves.

Every loss encountered – great and small, every fight endured, killed a little more and a little more of her until there was nothing left to kill.

In the end there was simply too much pain, too much that couldn't be unknown. It was all too much to bring into this new world, into this new life.

Her final words were to the point, "Please share my story," she requested, "So people can better understand this misunderstood disease. And more importantly, so those who are suffering know that they are not alone."

She couldn't help but add, however, that I should also relay the following message to a great number of her old friends and acquaintances with both middle fingers in the air and a smile:

Go fuck yourselves.

When those people come back and try to explain themselves, she made sure to remind me that David Silver put it best when he said, "It doesn't matter what you say about someone once they're gone. What matters is how you treat them when they're still here…."

I guess you can quote us on that.

She always knew the risks, even as a child. If she pushed herself far enough, if she climbed high enough, one day she might fall.

Well she fought until she couldn't see straight and she walked until the soles of her shoes were paper-thin. She pulled herself up over and over, until her palms bled from the bootstraps pressing against her skin.

It was time… time to stop climbing, time to rest, time to let go.

With the last of her strength, she pulled me out of that dark thick knee-high mud filled tunnel, then turned around and said goodbye.

So I took down her facebook page, deleted all the people off her phone, replaced her number. I went to court, stood in front of a judge and changed her name. I got rid of her driver's license, her bank account, her social security card.

She died at the young age of twenty-one.

...And as for me? Well, most days I'd be happy with the simplistic and quiet. I now imagine peaceful things for my life, like moving to the Midwest, maybe starting a bee farm, learn how to make honey. Most days I am very much aware that I am just a child. I want to go somewhere where I can play in the snow, I want to sneak out in the middle of the night and run on rooftops, swing on swings. When nobody is home, I wrestle with Junior. I have bite marks and bruises all over my arms in the shape of his teeth. I jump on my bed. I scream at the top of my lungs.

I still have that beautiful photograph she took of the cars decaying in the grass. And even though it is the photo that started this all, somehow, it still always makes me smile.

My name is Natalie London and this is the unexpected story of how *I* became free.

EPILOGUE

I close my eyes and see the rows of lights shining down on me that night. I could not wait anymore. I could not just watch the beauty fly by with my feet on the floor. The California wind rushing by the closed windows of my room, was simply not enough. I walked up those steep black steps in the middle of the show, closed my eyes, feeling what seemed like all the lights of the world flash to the bass line that rose up through my feet. I walked up to that stage, next to the thousands of black wires running full of music, the stars were out in this canyon, the stars shone down on a thousand soothed faces while the music wrapped itself around me. I lived in it. And in a moment, through the lens of my cheap plastic throw away camera, I snapped the picture.

I can still see it when I close my eyes.
I can still feel the glow against my face,

Filling me with light.

27103337R00151

Made in the USA
San Bernardino, CA
09 December 2015